COTTAGE PROJECTS

Charles Long

D1530573

Warwick Publishing

Toronto   Los Angeles

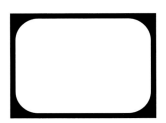

All images in a TV box (left) are video stills from the television series Cottage Country broadcast on CBC television in Canada and the Outdoor Life network in the United States.

ISBN 1-895629-75-6

Published by:
Warwick Publishing Inc., 24 Mercer Street, Toronto, Ontario M5V 1H3
Warwick Publishing Inc., 1424 N. Highland Avenue, Los Angeles, CA 90027

Distributed by:
Firefly Books Ltd., 3680 Victoria Park Avenue, Willowdale, Ontario M2H 3K1

Design: Diane Farenick

All photographs courtesy of Heather Halfyard, with the exception of the Cottage Chair (pages 6-13), courtesy of Greg Fess.

Printed and bound in Canada

COTTAGE
PROJECTS

TABLE OF CONTENTS

COTTAGE CHAIR

TOOLS

jigsaw

spokeshave or surform

sander: belt or orbital

table saw

   if ripping 1" stock to width

clamps

drill, bits, and driver

utility knife

putty knife and filler

HARDWARE

#8 flathead screws

   1 ¼"   38

   2 ½"   16

   3"   4

¼" carriage bolts

   2 ½"   4

   3"   4

washers

   8

nuts

   8

LUMBER

We used red cedar for this chair. Pine is often cheaper than cedar, but it is also more vulnerable to rot. What you save on lumber, you might have to spend on paint or preservative.

MINIMUM QUANTITIES

2 x 4

   5' front legs (2)

   arm blocks (4)

⁵⁄₄ x 6 "decking"

   20' seat supports (2)

   back braces (2)

   back legs (2)

   arms (2)

1 x 3

   40' back slats (6)

   seat slats (13)

This outdoor classic has been around so long that even the name has taken root. Whether you call it a Muskoka chair, Adirondack chair, or Algonquin chair depends on where you sit. Little differences in design make it more or less comfortable, but the basics common to all the variations suggest that this is truly a "no-name" chair.

The essential elements are wide armrests to hold refreshments, a contoured seat for

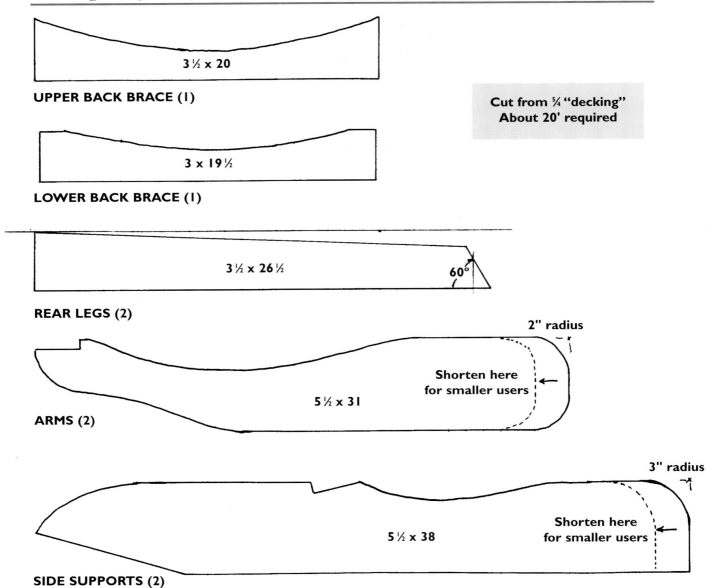

3½ x 20

UPPER BACK BRACE (1)

Cut from ¾ "decking"
About 20' required

3 x 19½

LOWER BACK BRACE (1)

3½ x 26½   60°

REAR LEGS (2)

2" radius

Shorten here
for smaller users

5½ x 31

ARMS (2)

3" radius

Shorten here
for smaller users

5½ x 38

SIDE SUPPORTS (2)

comfort, a high back to rest your head and sloped enough to snooze in. The plain, rugged construction takes the worry out of dragging it around the lawn and leaving it out in the rain.

Transfer the pattern for each piece to the lumber. For the curved arms and supports, mark a grid along the edge of the board and measure the distance from the edge at several

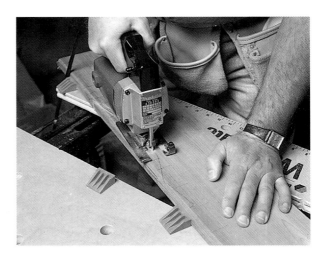

SEAT SLATS

| 1 ¾ x 19 ½ " | **(6 or 7)** |

| 1 x 19 ½ " | **(4)** |

**Cut from 1" lumber
20' clean 1 x 6**

| 2 x 19 ½ " | **(1 or 2)** |

| 2 ½ x 19 ½ " | **(1)** |

Shape notches against the actual curve of the back

(6) BACK SLATS

| 2 ½ x 36" | **Shape ends →
after assembly** |

| 3 ½ x 19 ½ " | **Shorten here ←
for smaller users** |

**Cut from 2" lumber
About 5' required**

FRONT ARM BLOCKS

REAR ARM BLOCKS

points along the curve. Connect the dots, free-hand, and score the line with a knife.

Use a jigsaw to rough out one piece, then use that as the pattern to trace the matching piece, first with pencil and then a knife. Scoring the line prevents the splinters that the jigsaw might otherwise kick up. Clamp the matching pieces together and trim the paired

If you have a table saw, you can rip the slats from any random width 1" lumber. Avoid weak knots, especially in the middle of the seat. If you have a lot of heavyweight company, you might prefer to switch to ¾" lumber for the slats as well as the supports.

Budget builders will look at the plans and see that it is almost possible to cut the ¾" pieces from two 8' lengths of decking. What the plans don't show are knots. Skimping on the lumber inevitably means ending up with a weak knot where you need some strength, or worse, a rock-hard knot where you have to sink a screw. Buy an extra board or two and lay out the pattern to avoid the awkward spots.

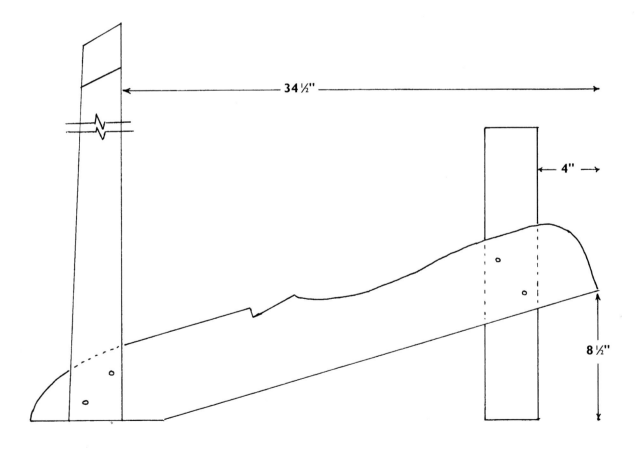

Layout of left-side assembly

Front leg "outside" the seat support; rear leg "inside" the seat support, insert bolts from the outside, washer and nut on the inside

edges with a spokeshave, surform, or sander. Finishing them side by side ensures that the two supports will match.

Assembly is easier if you draw a layout of the back leg, front leg, and side support on a large scrap of plywood or paneling—anything with a square factory edge from which to measure. You can clamp the pieces right to the pattern, so they don't wriggle around while you drill the ¼" bolt holes.

The two side supports may be the same shape, but they'll end up on different sides of the chair, and that will matter when we attach the legs. Mark one support "right" and the other "left," then mark the "inside" and "outside" of each. The front legs go on the outside of the supports, the rear legs on the inside. Also, remember to keep the heads of the bolts on the outside and the nuts on the inside.

Attach the four blocks which will support the arms. The front blocks sit flush with the tops of the front legs. The rear blocks are positioned at the same height to make the arms level. If you shorten the front leg for a smaller user, remember to lower the back arm block to the same height. Clamp each block in place and fasten it with two screws (2 ½" #8s will do at the back, but you'll need 3" screws to attach the blocks to the thicker front legs). Predrill each screw hole—especially with cedar—and countersink the heads for a nicer finish.

Stand up the two side assemblies, set the lower back brace across the notches, and attach one end with a 2 ½" screw. Now carefully check the spacing between the two side

supports. They should be 19" apart (outside to outside) for the whole length of the support. Check that the legs are vertical and the two side assemblies are squared with one another. It takes a little fiddling since the "chair" is now at its most wobbly state. However, wobbly also means that the leans and squints are still easy to straighten.

Satisfied? Okay, screw in the free end of the lower back brace. You'll notice that there's a little overlap at each end. The brace, like the seat slats, is cut about ¼" too long at

each end. That's so we can sand the end grains even at the finish.

The ends of the upper brace will overlap the leg tops by even more. The important thing is to keep the two back legs the same distance apart, top and bottom. Fasten one end of the brace with a 2 ½" screw, wiggle the other leg around until the two legs are parallel and vertical, then screw on the loose end of the brace. Attach a seat slat at the front of the chair to help hold the assembly in place while we work on the back.

The back slats on the pattern are 36" long. That's likely longer than you'll need, but we'll trim them at the end. For now, just turn each slat so the bad (trimmable) end sticks up. Now, too, is the time to sand all the edges of the back slats and seat slats. Stack the common widths on edge, clamp them together, and "gang" finish them with the belt sander.

Align the edge of the first back slat with the end of the curve on the lower brace and attach it with a single 1 ¼" screw. Then slide the top of the slat over until it's flush with the end of the upper brace and screw it there. Attach the slat on the far side the same way. Screw the four middle slats to the bottom brace, then fan them out and space them by eye.

Start the seat at the front with a 1 ¾" slat, flush with the bottom of the seat support. Here, where we're screwing into the end grain of the seat support, use a longer 2" screw, then switch to a 1 ¼" screw along the top. Let the slats stick out a little at either end, and space them by eye. The narrow 1" slats make a better job of rounding the tight front curve; four of them should get you to the front legs. The next two slats (1 ¾" wide) will have to be cut exactly 19" long to fit between the legs.

The awkward cut is at the very back. Hold the 2 ½" slat against the curve and mark the contours where it meets the back. No need to cut the entire curve. A little fitting at each end is fine. Whittle away the notches and screw this back slat in place before filling in the rest of the seat with 2" or 1 ¾" slats, depending on the spacing.

The arms fasten with two 2 ½" screws at the front and two at the back. At the back, one screw goes down into the supporting block, and one comes through the leg from the inside.

Ready for a trial sit? Lean back and—just before you fall asleep—pencil a mark just above your head. Later, get out the jigsaw and finish the top. Curve it, scallop it, or carve it, but cut above the mark if you want to rest your head.

Sand everything, especially the seat slats where they round the convex curves and expose their sharp edges. Fill the screw holes and finish with sealant, stain, or paint. Or, opt for naturally weathered cedar and relax for the rest of the day.

Acknowledgment: The author's plans for this cottage chair first appeared in **HOME AT HOME** *magazine, Winter 1996.*

PORCH SWING

LUMBER

A porch swing suffers a lot of yank and torque, even if you're just holding hands. Most of the stress is concentrated where the chain supports the wood. This is not the place for cedar or spruce. If the budget permits, use a hardwood, like oak. Or, carefully select from one of the tougher softwoods, like white pine. Avoid knotty pieces and incipient cracks.

2 x 4 pine:	2 bottom stringers, each 60" long	120"
	3 curved seat supports, each 26" long	78"
	2 front uprights, each 12" long	24"
	2 back uprights, each 26" long	52"
	3 back supports, top 55 ½" long	56"
	middle 51" long	51"
	bottom 51" long	51"
	2 armrests, each 24" long	48"
		480" = 40 linear feet

1 x 2 pine:	3 seat slats, each 51 ¼" long	13 linear feet
1 x 3 pine:	5 seat slats, each 51 ¼" long	
	12 back slats, each 23" long	36 linear feet
1 x 4 pine:	4 back slats, each 23" long	8 linear feet

A verandah is to summer what a fireplace is to winter—a place to relax and contemplate the sweet mysteries of life. And if one of life's mysteries is sitting beside you, the verandah is also about the most romantic spot at the cottage. Come on, even the most hard-boiled old do-it-yourselfer can remember a moonlit kiss on a summer verandah.

And if you can't remember such a kiss, you might want to add this old-fashioned porch swing to your moonlit places. It's just wide enough for two—without being too obvious—and is guaranteed to sweep you both off your feet. If you can't get a pucker out of this back porch beauty, you're going to need more than power tools and a project book to repair your love life.

We used a table saw to rip out the slats for the seat and the back, and to bevel the three back supports. If you don't have easy access to a table saw, simply select a variety of widths of 1" lumber for the slats, and rotate the square-edged back supports 15° instead of beveling them.

Likewise, we used a miter saw to cut all these pieces to length, and to cut the matching 15° angles on the arms. However, you can substitute a circular saw or even a handsaw.

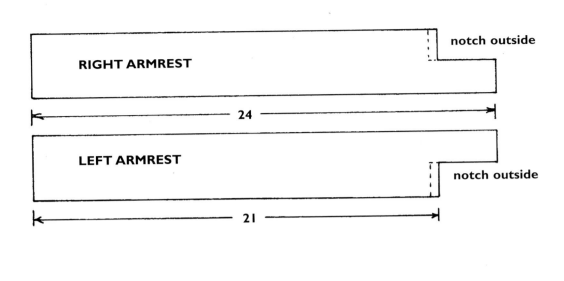

RIGHT ARMREST

notch outside

|← 24 →|

LEFT ARMREST

notch outside

|← 21 →|

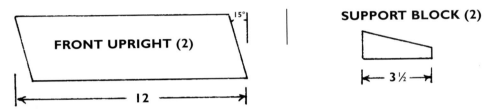

FRONT UPRIGHT (2)

15°

|← 12 →|

SUPPORT BLOCK (2)

|← 3½ →|

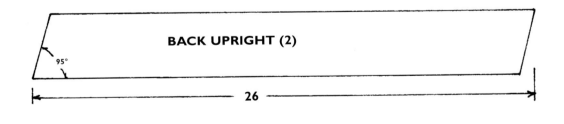

BACK UPRIGHT (2)

95°

|← 26 →|

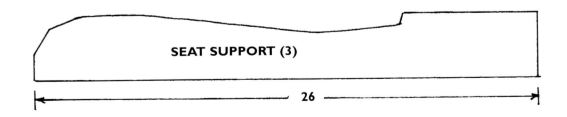

SEAT SUPPORT (3)

|← 26 →|

If you really, really have a lot of time on your hands, you could even cut the curved seat supports by hand. But a jigsaw will add speed and precision, ensuring that the three curved pieces match...and adding several days to your life.

In fact, if you really wanted to be Spartan about this, you could forget the curves and put a flat seat on the swing. You would, however, need a lot of moonlight to make up for a mistake like that. We copied these seat curves from a particularly relaxing cottage

FRAMEWORK AT END ASSEMBLY - FRONT VIEW

Top back support

← 55 ½" →

back upright

eye bolt

Middle back support

← 51" →

armrest

eye bolt

Bottom back support

front upright

← 51" →

seat support

eye bolt

Stringer

← 60" →

chair, fully expecting that the extra level of comfort will add another 15 minutes of romance to the evening.

Transfer the pattern from the grid to the 2 x 4s and rough out the curves with a jigsaw. You can improve on the match by aligning the three rough-cut seat supports in clamps or a vice and finishing them side by side. A rasp, spokeshave, or surform plane will erase the big discrepancies. A belt sander, run along all three edges simultaneously, will achieve a near perfect match.

The upright back supports aren't angled just for comfort. Note that the shorter front uprights are turned on the opposing angle. When we connect the front and back uprights with the armrest, together they form part of a truncated, upside-down triangle. A triangle—even a sort-of triangle turned upside down and with a point lopped off—is still a natural brace.

ASSEMBLE THE FRAME

Cut out all the supporting pieces and assemble the frame in the following order:

1. Lay out the three curved seat supports upside down (curved side down) on a flat surface. Position them parallel and spaced so that the two outer supports measure 51" from outside edge to outside edge; center the third support between them.

2. Lay the two 60" stringers across the seat supports. Set the stringers at right angles to the

**Attach the curved seat supports
to the bottom stringers.**

supports and clamp them if necessary.
Position one stringer flush with the back
(squared) ends of the three supports. Position
the other stringer 1" from the front ends of
the three supports. Both stringers should
project 4 ½" beyond the outer seat supports.

3. Fasten the stringers to the supports using
the 3" screws, two at each intersection.
Predrill and countersink the screws.

4. Turn the assembly right-side up, clamp
the four angled uprights in position, then
attach them with two carriage bolts
at each intersection.

5. Cut two short, angled support blocks
from 2 x 4 scrap and attach them to the
front uprights with a single screw each.

6. Attach the (51") bottom back support to the
seat supports. If you've beveled the back support, lay it flat on the seat supports and fitted
between the back uprights. If you haven't
beveled, rotate the back support so that its
front edge is flush with the front edges of the
uprights, and screw it through the uprights
and into the ends of the back support.

7. Cut a notch 1 ¾" wide at the back end of
each armrest, in order to fit them inside
the back uprights.

8. Attach each armrest with two screws at the
front and one into the upright at the back.

9. Fit the middle back support between the
back uprights and   attach it with a screw
at each end.

**Fit the arms inside the back upright, to allow
the chain to pass freely on the outside.**

10. Cut ¼" dados in the top back support, fit it over the ends of the back uprights, and attach with two screws at each end.

ADD THE SLATS

Start the back slats from the outside and work toward the center. If you bevel the tops of the slats 15°, you'll have a smoother joint

Large eye bolts in the upright allow the chains to pass through and stabilize the swing.

at the top, with less sanding. The first, wide slat needs a slight scallop along the outer edge, to allow the chain to pass freely. Space the rest of the slats about ½" apart. If you have to adjust the spacing or width of the slats, do it in the center and keep the uniform

symmetry on either side. Something different in the middle looks like a design feature. Anywhere else it might look like a mistake.

Start the seat slats at the front, using the narrower 2" slats to turn the corner and the wider slats along the gentler curve. Space them by eye, and if you must make an adjustment, save it for the last slat at the back. Do leave a gap between the last slat and the back, to avoid the possibility of tiny puddles.

Fill the screw holes with plugs or plastic filler. Then sand everything, especially those sharp-edged slats that turn the curve under the knees. Start with a #50 or #80 grit and work up to a #120.

Cut ¼" dados in the top back support and fit it over the back uprights.

HARDWARE

The hardware should all be coated or plated against corrosion. And make sure you get heavy, welded-link chain. It's no good sweeping her off her feet only to come crashing down because you decided to save 20 bucks by recycling the old dog chain.

8 eye bolts
> shank: at least ¼" diameter and 2" long
> ensure that the eye is wide enough to let the chain pass through

8 nuts
> ¼"

8 washers
> ¼"

2 eye bolts
> shank: ⅜" diameter, 6" long (approximately)
> the shank must be long enough to pass through the ceiling support

2 nuts
> ⅜"

2 washers
> ⅜"

2 chains
> each 30" long, welded links

2 chains
> each 90" long (approximately)
> have the chain cut at the store if you don't have a cutter

8 "quick" links or threaded connectors

8 carriage bolts
> ¼" diameter, 3 ½" long

8 nuts
> ¼"

8 washers
> ¼"

29 screws
> #8
> 3" long

80 screws
> #8
> 2" long

Use the narrower seat slats to round the curve at front.

SUSPENDERS YOU CAN COUNT ON

So far we have a comfy, but very low couch. To put a little swing in things, install the eye bolts in the bottom stringers and in the uprights. The bottom eyes are for support, the upper eyes for stability.

Pass the chains through the upper eyes, and attach them to the lower eyes with the threaded links. Then hook the short chain to the longer one with another threaded link. Don't worry about just where the two chains join; we'll adjust this connection at the end, for maximum comfort.

The most important connection is at the top, where the swing hangs from its supports. Not every ceiling will take the weight. And, if you have any doubts, this is the time to call in a professional.

There are several possibilities, depending

on how the roof was built and what sort of ceiling hides it. Somewhere up there are rafters (sloped) or joists (horizontal). They may be 2 x 6s or 2 x 8s, and they extend out from the wall to rest on a beam—a thicker, horizontal timber. The beam is likely supported on vertical posts. The best place to hang the swing is from the beam. If the beam is inconvenient, you can suspend the swing from two or more well-supported joists. In other words, don't fasten the two chains to a single joist, but turn the swing at right angles, so each side hangs from a different joist. If the ceiling is open, you can set a new beam across the tops of the joists, fix the beam in position, and hang the swing from the beam. If you use the joists in any way, check the support at the wall. The joist should extend through the siding and rest on the framing inside the wall.

Here, we installed a new 6 x 6 beam and put two ⅜" eye bolts completely through it. A large washer on the top side ensures we won't pull the eye bolt out. And two nuts, one tightened against the other, will keep them from wiggling loose.

Set the swing up on sawhorses, milk crates, or something to hold the weight off the ground while you connect the long chains to the eye bolts with the threaded "quick" links. Now remove the milk crates—or whatever—

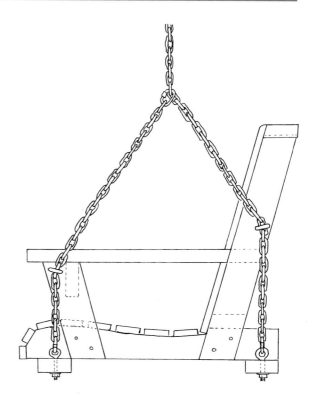

Suspend the chains from a solid beam.

and check to see if the swing sits level and at a comfortable height from the floor. Adjustment is as simple as changing the top connecting link.

The final adjustment depends on whether you want to sit up prim and proper or lean back and relax. Test drive the swing, with a companion if possible, then adjust the link where the short chain connects to the longer one. A higher connecting link will tilt the seat back, a lower connection will tilt it forward.

Leave fresh lumber to weather for a week or two before you finish it. Then sand it again lightly and paint it or stain it.

POUTING STOOL

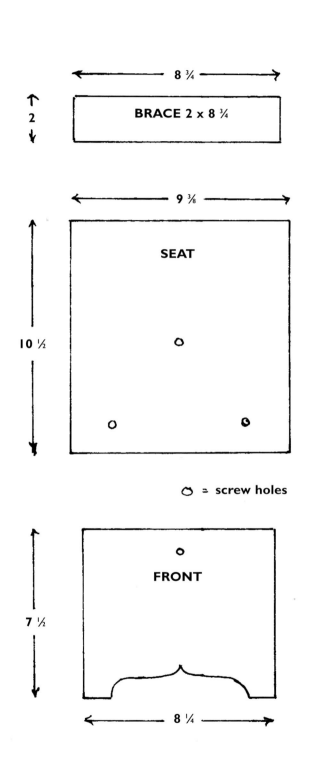

← 8 ¾ →

BRACE 2 x 8 ¾

2

← 9 ⅜ →

SEAT

10 ½

⭕ = screw holes

FRONT

7 ½

← 8 ¼ →

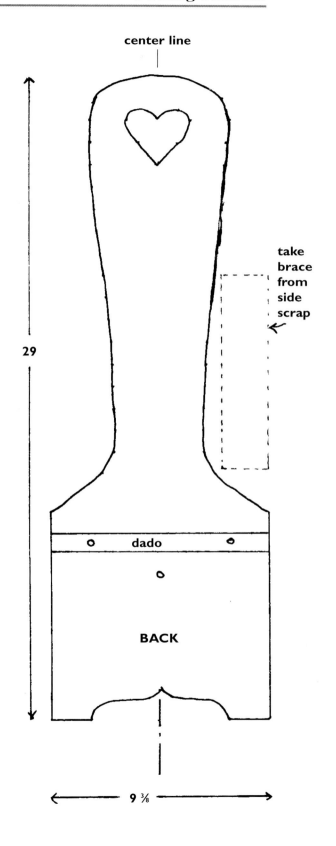

center line

take
brace
from
side
scrap

29

dado

BACK

← 9 ⅜ →

Trace the pattern onto the back board.

Childhood is a time when simple things suffice. And maybe that's why grownups are so attracted to cottages. It's our chance to return to the simple things, too. Which is certainly one of the pleasures of making bits and pieces of furniture for the cottage. It's supposed to be simple, plain, straightforward, nothing fancy. Like the pouting stool.

Tradition calls it a pouting stool because that's where little people sit while waiting for the tears to dry and the smiles to come back. Construction is purposely simple and purposely small. It's the one piece of furniture we want the kids to grow out of, not into.

If and when they do outgrow it, the stool will make an attractive plant stand. It will stand alone or hang on the wall, perhaps for that weeping fig or pot of impatiens.

One 4' length of 1 x10" pine takes care of material requirements. Working with single

Cut out the heart with a jigsaw.

Cut a dado (or shallow groove) to hold the seat.

angle cut. The back can be copied from the plans included here. Or, make your own pattern by folding a long piece of paper (or thin cardboard) in half, lengthwise. Cut half a heart and half of the bottom scallop from the creased edge. Cut one side curve from the uncreased edges. When you unfold the pattern, the two sides will match, symmetrically.

Trace the pattern onto the board and cut it out with a jigsaw. The bottom scallop from the back piece will also serve to trace the front piece. Notice, however, that the front piece is slightly narrower than the back. If you have trouble centering the pattern on the board (which may be the case if you're using floppy paper for the pattern), draw a center line the length of the board and align the point of the heart and the point of the bottom scallop with the center line on the board.

If you follow the pattern here, there will be just enough scrap left over from the back to provide a 2" brace for under the seat.

Now cut a dado across the back piece, starting 7 ½" from the bottom and exactly as wide as the seat is thick. Do not take the width of the dado from these or any other plans because the width of the dado should match the exact thickness of your lumber, and that depends on where you bought it and how dry it is. Nominal 1" lumber is usually

boards that wide takes some care, however. Now matter how closely you inspect it at the lumber yard, cupping or warping can start as soon as you get it out of the pile.

You can fight the warps by buying the best kiln-dried lumber, by keeping it in the shade, and by stacking it flat with sticks between boards so air circulates evenly on all sides. It's not water that warps lumber so much as it is uneven drying.

If that seems like too much trouble for a project as simple as this one, buy the wide, laminated panels sold for shelving, or make your own by joining narrower boards edge to edge with glue. Alternate the arcs of the visible end grain to keep the little warps from joining forces.

Cut the three main pieces from the 1 x10 board or panel. The seat is a simple right

**Center the brace,
then secure it with glue
and a screw at each end.**

¾" thick, but it can vary by as much as an ⅛" either way. That doesn't sound like much, but it's enough to spoil the joint.

Regardless of whether you're using a router, table, radial-arm, or miter saw, set the depth of the cut at less than half the thickness of the wood. A quarter of an inch is plenty. Make the two outside cuts first, then kerf the middle waste and clean it out with a narrow chisel.

Try the seat in the dado. It should slide in snugly, with almost no wobble. The dado joint is much stronger here than a simple butt joint. Better still, it helps to square up the pieces and keep the seat in position while you glue and screw the rest together.

Predrill the screw holes in the positions shown. If you have a counter-sink bit, use it so that the screw heads can be set below the surface.

The order of assembly is important to keep the pieces square with a minimum of fuss. Start with the brace. Smear glue on one end (ordinary carpenter's glue is best) and hold the brace exactly on the center line of the back piece, flush with the bottom edge of the dado. Then drive in the screw from the back.

Glue the other end of the brace and screw it to the front piece. Again, hold the brace on the center line and flush with the top of the front piece as you set the screw.

If you've cut the ends of the brace square, it will hold the front and back square. The stool is still seatless but able to stand on its own.

Now slobber glue into the dado and along the tops of the brace and the front. Shove the seat into the dado and adjust it so

Sand everything, finishing with a #120 grit.

that the back corners are flush at the sides. Drive the screws through the back and into the seat. Then—before setting any more screws—check the alignment of the brace and the front, to ensure that they are centered under the seat. There will still be enough play in the brace attachments to make any necessary adjustments.

When it all lines up, drive the three screws through the seat into the brace and front.

Tightening the screws will inevitably squish glue out of the joints. Resist the urge to wipe it all off right away. Wiping smears the wet glue into the porous surface of the wood and affects the finish. You'll have to do a lot of sanding, in the most difficult corners, or suffer the unsightly smears as permanent blotches under the finish. Only painting will cover the smears. If, instead, you leave the glue to gel (firm but not hard), you can scrape it off later and have much less sanding to do.

Fill the screw holes with wooden plugs or plastic filler. And leave everything to dry until it's hard enough to sand. Finish with #120 grit paper and clean up the dust. Then seal the surface with stain, or a primer coat if you're going to paint.

Once the surface is sealed and dry, you can add a personal touch with stencils or découpage. We chose a duck to give this stool a cottage look, but there are hundreds of

Thick stencil creams are less likely to bleed under the edge of the stencil.

other patterns available from the paint department or hobby shop.

Several coats of clear finish will protect the decoration from wear and tear.

Acknowledgment: The author's plans for "Pouting Stool" also appear in HOME AT HOME *magazine, Spring 1997.*

GATEPOST

irections to the cottage get a little complicated when the pavement turns to dirt and the road signs disappear. You can direct would-be visitors to watch for the "first big stump past the swampy bit...you can't miss it!" But lots of people will. And that could mean more than a lost visitor. If you're expecting a fire truck or an ambulance, a missed direction could mean trouble.

Which is why careful cottagers hang a sign on the gatepost. Or—in the absence of a working gate and gatepost—at least something solid to hold the sign.

BASE

There is no need to dig a foundation below the frostline. It's easier to support a simple structure like this on a "floating" concrete pad. If it does heave a little with frost, it will move as one unbroken piece on its concrete raft and settle back more or less where it started. A pushy root or a soft pocket of subsidence might cause another kind of tilt, but most such problems are near the surface. Open a hole about 3' square and 12" deep. Level the bottom of the excavation, down to a flat base of undisturbed subsoil.

Six inches of crushed stone will half-fill the hole and provide all the drainage

A poured concrete pad works like a raft, moving with the frost but carrying its cargo intact.

we need. Before you dump in stone, however, consider the pros and cons of an eventual light on top of the gatepost. It might help a visitor in the dark, but—on the other hand—it does look a little suburban. It might deter vandals, but it does require power from the cottage. Can't decide? Neither could we. So, for a few dollars worth of electrical conduit, we left all options open. If we later decide on a light, we can push the wire through the conduit and dig the ditch back to the cottage. If we decide against the light, we can cut off the top of the conduit and plug the hole. Frankly, including the conduit is less trouble than building a family consensus on whether or not to have a light.

So, dump in the crushed stone around the conduit and tamp it down in layers: 2-3" of stone then stomp it down; another couple of inches and stomp it down.

Construct a simple form of 2 x 6s: four boards, each 36" long, nailed at the corners. Set it on the crushed rock base and level it. Then shovel in dirt or rock around the outside to brace it in position. Make sure the conduit is precisely in the center of the form.

Fill the form with concrete. The simplest way to make concrete in small quantities is with bagged premix. Just add water and stir. You'll

Screed off the excess concrete with a board.

need about 12 bags for the base. Prod the mixture into the corners of the form with a shovel, working out the air pockets. When the form is full, strike off the excess by sliding a board back and forth across the top of the form. Then check that the conduit is still perfectly plumb. Cover the concrete with plastic and leave it overnight to harden.

STONE

In the morning, we marked a 28" square on the surface of the concrete. This is the outline for the first course of stone. More importantly, it establishes the four corner references, which we'll have to extend right to the top. Now, I know that you and I would never drop mortar, but if you're forced to use a less fastidious helper, drive a small concrete nail at each corner to help you find the reference later.

Slap a thick bed of mortar into the 28" square, keeping the mortar an inch or two back from the line.

Select four stones with reasonably square

corners and roughly the same height. The cornerstones don't have to have perfect edges. They can be rough or rounded. But the two faces of the stone that form the corner should be at right angles to one another.

Set the cornerstones in the mortar, aligning them with the marks on the base. Make sure the two exposed faces rise more or less vertically. You might have to prop the cornerstone up with a shim (or small rock wedge) from behind. If it sits only slightly askew, hold it in position and tap the top gently with a hammer to settle it into proper alignment.

When the corners are in place, fill in the four faces between them. Again, try to select stones that match the heights of the cornerstones. Tap them into the mortar, and align each face with the corners.

You can square corner stones with hammer and chisel. Keep the shaft of the chisel upright, and the blade aligned with the intended cut.

Set the corner stones first

TOP VIEW OF ONE COURSE IN PROGRESS

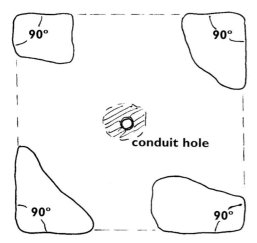

Set corner stones

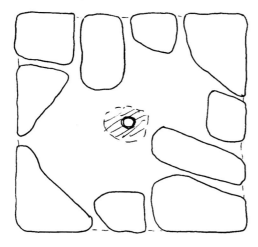

Fill in faces between the corners

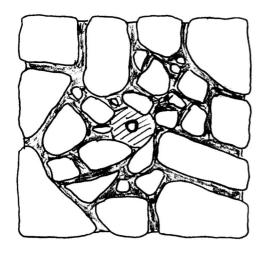

Fill in with rubble behind and stuff mortat in the gaps

Now, fill in behind the faces with any sort of rubble. It doesn't matter what the backfill looks like or what shape it is. But, once again, try to match the height of adjacent stones. You don't have to fill right against the conduit. Indeed, a small hollow at the core saves material and helps ensure you don't push the conduit out of plumb. You can stuff in wads of paper (tear up an empty cement bag) to keep mortar from falling down the hole.

When the course (one layer of stones) is complete, work mortar between the stones from the top. At the back you can be sloppy. But go carefully nearer the face. If you over-stuff the joint and it oozes wet mortar down the front of the stones, it can stain the rocks and look a mess. If mortar does bulge out of the joint, don't try to push it back in. Not yet. For now, just slice off the excess and let it fall.

If you can't bring the course up to a common height with a single layer of stones, fill the low areas with thinner stones to try for a level top.

The second course proceeds just like the first, with one important exception:

1. Lay down a bed of mortar.

2. Set the corners, and align them with the marks on the base below. Don't align the corner with the stone below (it may be rounded or uneven enough to mislead you). Aim at the base reference, and use a level or plumb bob, not the naked eye.

Keep the corners vertical from reference marks on the base.

Use a narrow trowel to force the mortar back into the joint and smooth it.

Cover the gap between the form and the stones with wooden spacers and plastic

3. Fill in the faces between the corners.

4. Fill in with rubble behind.

5. Stuff mortar between the stones.

6. Bring the course up to a common height.

The important exception in the second and succeeding courses is to place each rock so that there are no continuous vertical joints. Each stone should rest on at least two stones below, so that all the vertical gaps are bridged. This strengthens the wall and makes it more aesthetically pleasing. This is also why we took such care to try to finish the previous course at a common height. If any rock sticks up higher than its neighbor, it is more difficult to bridge the gap between them. We would have to find a rock with an unnatural matching "step" in its underside or fill in beside the big rock to bring its neighbors up to height.

A couple of hours after starting, check the early mortar joints. By now the mortar should be getting dry. You can still cut it with the trowel, but it crumbles and falls instead of running and smearing. Use the point of the trowel to slice away the excess bulges. Then, with a narrow trowel or a wet (gloved) finger, force the mortar back into the joint. Push hard as you slide the trowel along the joint, thus leaving a smooth, slightly recessed joint.

CAP

When the post looks almost high enough, level off the last course and prepare to pour a concrete cap. The cap both ties the top of the post together and sheds the rain.

The trick is to build a form wider than the post, leaving a drip edge. Exact dimensions depend on the size of the post and on how irregular the faces of the rocks are.

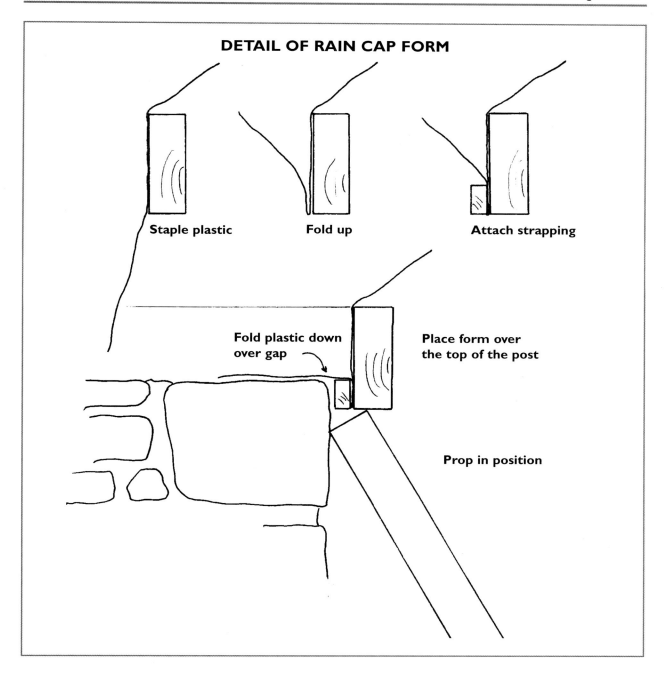

DETAIL OF RAIN CAP FORM

Staple plastic

Fold up

Attach strapping

Fold plastic down over gap

Place form over the top of the post

Prop in position

For this 28" post, built of reasonably uniform sandstone, we started with four 2 x 6s, each 31 ½" long. When we lapped the corners and screwed it together, we got a box measuring 30" inside. That would leave a 1" projection all around the perimeter of our post. It would also leave a 1" gap for the wet concrete to leak down the face of the stones. Which is where the strips of plastic and the 1 x 2 strapping enter the picture.

Staple a strip of heavy plastic to the inner face of each side of the form. Fold it up at the

Level the form and prop it solidly in place

Carefully work the wet concrete into all the corners.

MORTAR

Mixing mortar is the trickiest part of this job. If you're using bagged premix, the directions sound simple: Just add clean water and stir. The problem is that there's no exact formula for how much water. It depends on the humidity in the bag, the temperature outside, and the mood of the gods.

A hoe makes a reasonable ad hoc mixer; and a steel-pan wheelbarrow provides an ideal mixing vessel. Make a crater in the pile of dry mix, pour in a quart or two of clean water, then pull the rim of the crater into its little lake. All the free water will disappear into damp lumps of sand, with plenty of dry stuff left around the edges. Chop it up with the hoe, and make another crater and a much smaller lake. Mix it with vigor and add even smaller amounts of water, until every speck of dry stuff has been folded into a uniformly damp slab of mud that stands up like freshly mashed potatoes.

The usual beginner's mistake is to add too much water at the end. The difference between an almost perfect mix and unusable soup is about half a cup of water. Add smaller and smaller amounts as you mix. If it crumbles, it's still a tad too dry. If it folds and slices in slick-faced slabs that slide off the trowel and hold their shapes, it's perfect. If it splatters and flows, you've gone a drop too far. Throw it out and start again.

bottom and screw a length of strapping over the fold (see diagram). Place the form over the top of the post and hold it there with props. The strapping fills most of the gap between the form and the stone. The plastic flaps down over the rest. Given the irregular faces of the stones, it would be impossible to block the entire gap with wood. Indeed, there were several places where we had to whittle away at the strapping to accommodate the bumps. Caulk any potential leaks in the overlapping plastic, level the form, check the props, and pour in the concrete.

Pouring the cap is just like pouring the

base, except you need a little less concrete and a little more attention to the finish. Mound the concrete slightly higher in the middle and shape it roughly to shed the rain. Then leave it alone for an hour or so before you apply the trowel.

Pass the trowel over the surface in overlapping arcs. A little gentle pressure will settle the pebbles below the surface and bring up a damp skim of sand and cement. Beware of starting too early or troweling too long. Either will raise an excess of water. Finish with an edging trowel if possible, then cover the whole thing with plastic and leave it to cure for three days.

Finally, unscrew the forms, cut away the plastic, and attach the number, the name, or whatever you need by way of ID. You can drill holes in mortar, or in soft stone, with a special masonry bit and an ordinary drill. For harder stone, you may have to rent a small "hammer" drill to bore the holes for the screw anchors.

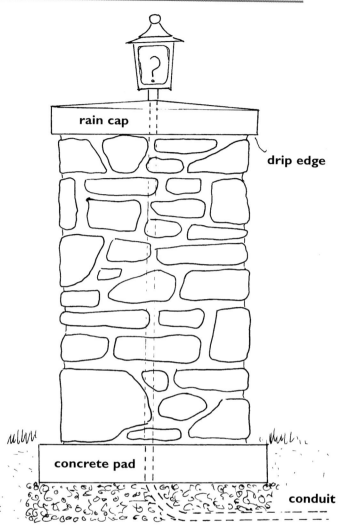

rain cap

drip edge

concrete pad

conduit

crushed rock base

An edging trowel leaves a slightly rounded lip on the cap.

Cut away the plastic and you're ready to finish with a light on top or a fancy number at the front.

PICNIC TABLE

90"

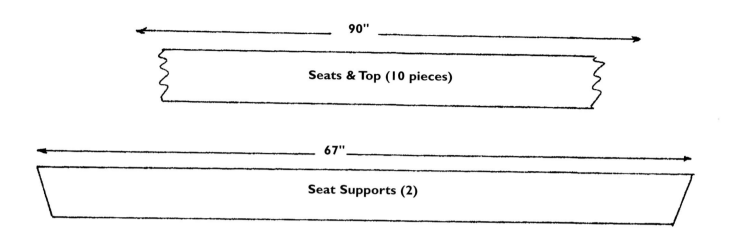

Seats & Top (10 pieces)

67"

Seat Supports (2)

MATERIALS

2 x 6 cedar
8' long
16 pieces

¼" carriage bolts
3 ½" long
16

nuts
16

washers
16

#8 flathead screws
2 ½" long
68

36"

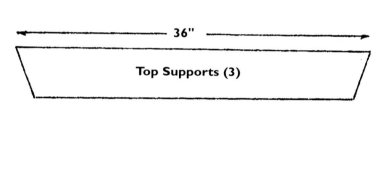

Top Supports (3)

30½"

Legs (4)

35"

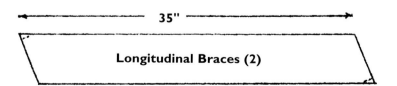

Longitudinal Braces (2)

Somebody will undoubtedly stick a photograph on this page, but it will be superfluous. When I say "picnic table," you'll know exactly what I mean, without looking at any picture. The picnic table is so simple, so practical, and so plain that there is only one basic design. Nothing has improved on the prototype.

We work on it, play on it, sometimes even eat on it. It's always there. And, since "always" includes the bad weather days, the poor old picnic table takes a beating. Sooner or later the boards weather and crack, bolts loosen, seats sag, and legs begin to wobble. Sound familiar? Well, at least we know when it's time to make a new one, even if we don't know how to make a better one.

Simplicity begins at the lumber yard, where the materials list comprises one size of bolt, one size of screw, and one size of lumber. The lumber of choice is 2 x 6 cedar, simply because it is naturally rot resistant. Pine costs less, but what you save on lumber you'll spend on paint or preservative. You might also see picnic tables made of pressure-treated lumber, but those are for the families with perfect children, the ones who never lick spills.

You'll need a tape measure, a portable circular saw, and a ¼"

CUTTING JIG

Use a piece of scrap lumber or plywood, about 8" wide and at least 12" long. Cut the jig angle (in this case, 70°) on the table saw. Or, mark the angle with a protractor and cut it freehand. Screw on a 1 x 2 scrap, flush with the long edge. Put the jig on the board to be cut, pull it firmly against the far side of the board with one hand, and run the saw along the angle with the other hand.

drill. If the drill also has drivers for screws and nuts, you'll save an hour of hand work and a couple of blisters. That's basic. For a deluxe finish, add a countersink bit, a belt sander, and a utility knife to your tool kit.

The handiest tool is a homemade jig (see the box) to mark all the angled cuts and to guide the circular saw on the only angle you'll need: 70°. Set up the jig angle on a table saw, or lay it out with a protractor. There's no magic in setting up at exactly 70°; a couple of degrees either way won't make much difference. The important thing is that all the angles match. So prepare a clean, straight guide-edge on the jig and use it for every cut.

A simple home-made jig guides the saw to make every angled cut the same.

Sort the lumber according to use. Save the four best pieces for the seats—you don't want to sit on a splinter or a sticky knot. The top will take six of the next-best pieces, reasonably straight and no big knots. Warped lumber doesn't look so bad in shorter lengths, so put the worst of it aside for legs and supports. Finally, plan to make the table just a little shorter than the lumber. A 90" table from 8' lumber, for example, leaves 6" excess on every board—enough to trim off most of those ragged ends.

Begin by cutting out the legs and horizontal supports as shown in the pattern. Keep in mind that you'll be driving a lot of screws into the top edges of the supports. Lay it out so that the supports have the fewest possible knots where the screws will go.

The easiest way to cut the angles is to clamp the board to a sawhorse or secure it in a vise. Pull the jig firmly against the far side of the board with one hand, and run the saw along the angle of the jig with the other hand.

Lay out the end assembly on a flat surface, with clamps to hold the legs and supports in place. Position the pieces carefully so that the horizontal supports intersect the legs at the correct heights (see pattern). If you have one of those chromosomes that compels you to make lists and do crossword puzzles in pencil, you can double-check the layout using the cutting jig—all intersecting angles should be 70°. With the two legs and two supports in position and tightly clamped, drill ¼" holes for the eight bolts. Position the bolt holes on diagonals as shown.

Tap in the bolts from the outside, i.e., from the support side of the assembly. Add a washer to the other end of the bolt, against the leg. And then a nut. Notice that the nuts

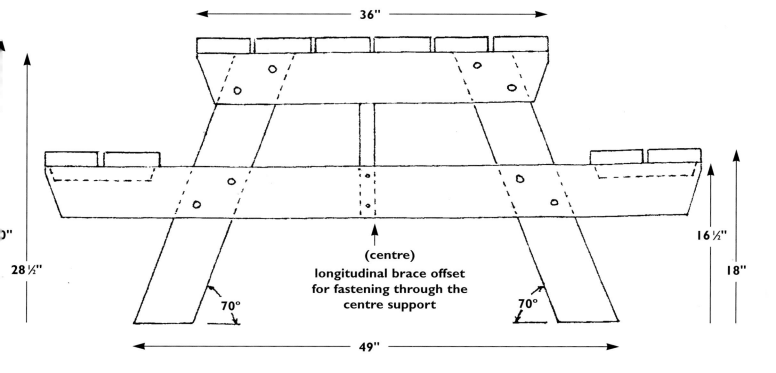

(centre)
longitudinal brace offset
for fastening through the
centre support

end up under the table (not unlike some picnics). Tighten the nuts until the washers compress the wood. The finished end assembly will look a little like a fat, flat-topped, capital A. The splayed legs brace the assembly against any seat-to-seat wobble.

Lay out the second end assembly in the same way. But check the final position of the pieces by laying the first, completed assembly over the top. The two should match, in all dimensions and angles. Clamp the pieces of the second assembly and bolt it together as before.

Tying the two ends together with seat boards and top is easy if you have lots of hands to hold the ends upright. If you are working alone, start with one end assembly and two top boards. Hold the assembly more or less upright with one hand. With the other hand, pick up one end of a top board and lay it across the top support. Leave about 12" projecting beyond the support and set the outer edge of the board flush with the end of the support. Let the end assembly lean in a bit, so

that the top board (with one end still on the ground) is roughly square with the end assembly. Hold it or clamp it, and drive in a screw.

Now that it's self-propping, attach the other top board to the other end of the top support. The two boards are now twin props, holding up the end assembly. Raise the props off the ground and stand the other end assembly in place beneath them. Position the two end assemblies so that they're parallel to one another, perfectly upright, and square to the two top boards. Check to be sure that both end assemblies have their horizontal supports on the outside and their legs on the inside. Then fasten the free ends of the top boards. It wobbles from end to end, but it stands alone.

Attach the horizontal center support beneath the top boards. Then add the two longitudinal braces. If you offset the longitudinal braces, setting them to either side of the center line, you can screw through the center support and into the ends of the braces. The length and angled ends of the longitudinal

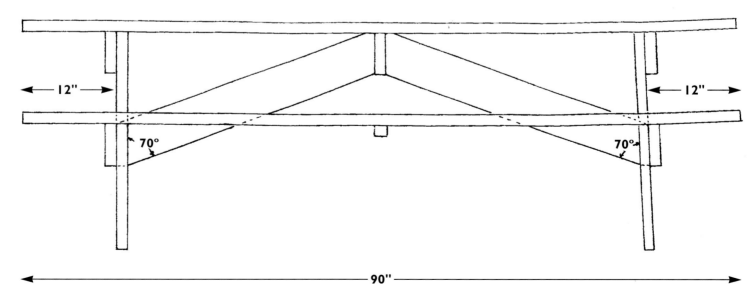

**The end assembly provides
support for seats and top.**

braces may vary slightly, depending on how far apart you've placed the end assemblies. If you want to vary the pattern—for a longer table, for example—leave these braces a little long and mark the exact angles in place.

Likewise, the angled cut on the end of the brace will be greater than the 5 ½" width of the adjoining supports. In other words, when you abut the brace against the horizontal supports, there's a little point left over. You can leave the little points, trim them off, or rip the longitudinal braces to a 5" width on the table saw to make everything come out even.

Fastening the longitudinal braces will stop the end-to-end wobbles. It will also prevent any further adjustment of the legs. Make sure everything is square and the legs are vertical before you screw the longitudinals in place.

The remaining top boards and the four seat boards should be spaced about ½" apart. Much more than that risks tipping glasses in the cracks. Tighter cracks will guck up with crumbs. Use a spacer to keep the separations uniform. And use two screws at each support, six screws per board.

For speed, measure a 12" projection on the good end of these boards and let the ragged ends stick out farther. You can trim them off to 12" after they're all in place. Why no more than a 12" projection? That's just wide enough for a skinny child, but too small for anybody heavy enough to tip the table by sitting outside the legs.

Attach 2 x 2 braces underneath the seats, in the middle. A heavyweight picnicker can bow a 2 x 6. But with the brace in place, the big guy would have to bow two 2 x 6s tied together.

Now trim off the ragged ends of the top. Use a long straightedge to mark the cut across all six boards. Then score the line with a utility knife to prevent the saw from pulling up splinters. Trim the seat ends the same way and sand absolutely everything, starting with #50 or #80 and finishing with a #120 grit. There will be bare legs and party dresses sliding along these seats.

New cedar looks—and smells—much too nice to cover up with paint or stain. But untreated wood, even cedar, will begin to discolor under the sun. It will discolor even faster if your fellow picnickers are prone to spills. We left this one outside for a year before sanding it down again and protecting it with a tough, alkyd stain that promises to resist the grease spots and catsup marks.

Acknowledgment: The author's picnic table plans and do-it-yourself instructions also appear in Harrowsmith Country Life, *May 1996.*

FLAGSTONE PATH

A flagstone path will fit in any of those places where the pitter-patter of feet has worn a rut in the grass, a rut that becomes a runnel of mud when it rains. The first rut to appear is the one leading from the parking spot to the cottage door. But pedestrian wear eventually shows wherever the human traffic funnels itself into narrow paths.

Here, for example, the route to the clothesline gradually bent itself into a skinny S as it skirted a spreading cedar. The beaten path clearly shows where the flagstones have to go. It would be possible, I suppose, to top such a path with concrete slabs or patterned pavers, but flagstone is always a more natural choice at the cottage. Not only does it belong to the landscape, but the rugged blocks invite a looser fit. A little casual irregularity that would spoil the tight geometry of interlocking brick looks right at home amongst these natural flagstones.

The simplest approach is to set some big, flat stones in the sod. They will, however, shift a little as frost expands the moist soil beneath or shift more than a little if they rest on a soft base of organic soil.

You can prevent the shifts, and resultant stubbed toes, by

laying the flagstones on a base of crushed rock. Water will drain away through the crushed rock, leaving nothing for the frost to expand. And passing feet, bikes, and wheelbarrows can't pound the stones any deeper into this compact base.

Start with the flagstones. You'll need stones that are flat on top (we'll bury any rounded bottoms in the base). And the bigger the better. Little stones will get kicked loose by the lawn mower or pushed into the ground. The larger slabs cover more area with fewer edges to fit. More importantly, the big ones are more stable. Like snowshoes, they distribute the weight over a wider area. How big? Think "snowshoe" and pick stones bigger than your foot.

For the most part, stone comes free in cottage country. If the ground wasn't covered in stone, it would likely be a farm and not a cottage. Don't pull stones out of the lake, however. You'd be destroying fish habitat and probably a few environmental regulations. Look in old fence rows, instead, and along highway cuttings.

If flat stone isn't readily available, you can buy it from a quarry or from a landscape center. Look for "Stone" in the Yellow

A long board, set across the tops of the grade stakes, represents the top of the path. Measure the depths of base materials from there

Pages. You'll want sandstone or limestone, which split naturally into flat slabs. And you'll want the nearest source you can find because the trucking will cost more than the stone. The cheapest way is to take your own truck or trailer to the quarry and load the stone yourself.

Calculate the surface area of the path and use that as your guide to the quantity required. This path, for example, is 16' long and a bit over 2' wide. That's 32 square feet,

Fit the stones like a giant jigsaw puzzle, starting with the biggest pieces at the ends and along the sides.

and it took 23 rocks to cover it. The average rock, obviously, was more than a foot square. Only the surface area counts. The thickness of the slabs is between you and your back.

The base materials—crushed stone and stonedust—will also come from the quarry. And, like the flagstones, the base materials will cost more to haul than to buy. You'll need a 4-6" depth of clear crushed stone (¾" or ⅞") and at least a 1" bed of stonedust. Calculate the volume (length x width x depth) for the area of the path, but don't cut

quantities too fine. If you have to get it delivered, a part load won't be much cheaper than a full load. Any leftovers can fill the potholes in the lane.

1. You can lay out a straight-edged path with string or "draw" a sweeping curve with a length of garden hose, as we've done here. A 2' width is plenty for a single walker on a utilitarian path to the clothesline or privy. A more social path, to the barbecue or the beach, should be at least twice that wide for side-by-side strolling. Mark the edges of the path with grade stakes every 3-4'. Drive in the stakes until the tops are the same height as the intended surface of the path. In general, the path should be level from side to side but rise and fall with the terrain along its length. If possible, don't let the surface of the path fall below the natural surface; it will only collect leaves, grass clippings, and water. Instead, keep the tops of the stakes about 2-3" higher than the ground around the path. Later, you can fill in along the raised edges with a little slope of excavated earth, which will allow the lawn mower over the edges and help with the drainage.

2. Excavate the area between the grade stakes. The object is to make room for the base materials and the flagstone. So start by estimating the thickness of your average flagstone. Then add an inch for the stonedust bed and another 4-6" for the

crushed stone base. Here, our stones were about 3" thick, so we excavated 8" below the tops of the grade stakes (3" + 1" + 4" = 8"). The other reason to excavate is to remove grass, roots, and any loose organic soil that would allow the path to settle. Ideally, the measured excavation ends neatly on an undisturbed bottom of subsoil. In the real world, excavators hit big rocks (leave them) and unexpected roots (remove them). If you do dig deeper than you have to, don't refill the dips with dirt. Your refills will eventually compact, allowing the path to sink. Instead, fill the uneven bottom with the crushed stone; that's why we estimated the depth of the crushed stone base at 4-6". We weren't being wishy-washy; we were simply expecting the unexpected in the bottom of most holes.

3. Now dump in some of the crushed stone, rake it level, and compact it with a hand tamper, a vibrating plate compactor, or a lawn roller. Then measure from the tops of the stakes and add another layer. Fill, rake, and compact in layers until the base is just high enough to leave room for the stonedust and flagstones. In this case, we

Better than a jigsaw puzzle — if a stone *almost* fits, you can knock off a bit to *make* it fit.

had to bring the base to within 4" of the stake tops to allow for a 1" dust bed and the 3" flagstones.

4. The stonedust layer is there to accommodate the lumpy bottoms of the flagstones. It's a leveler, a gap-filler. So the lumpier the bottoms on the flagstones, the more stonedust you will need. A 1" bed is enough for flat, uniform slabs, but leave more room if your flagstones are rough and uneven. If this is a budget job, you can substitute sand for stonedust. Sand is more readily available; stonedust provides more stability. Whatever you use, don't compact it. Rake it level and leave the rake marks on the surface.

5. Start with the largest stone and lay it in the busiest spot—where a gate or a step might concentrate the traffic. And set the heaviest stones along the edges, where weeding and mowing would work lighter stones loose.

6. Level each stone as you set it. The desired surface is defined by the grade stakes. So place a long, straight board from stake top to stake top: across the path, along the edges, or diagonally. The

top of the stone should just touch the bottom of the board. If the stone is too low, tip it up and add more stonedust. If the stone sits too high, tip it up, rake away some stonedust, and resettle the stone with a tap or a stomp. The stone's impression on the furrowed surface of the stonedust will show you where to add or remove the bedding material.

7. Fit the stones edge to edge. Like a jigsaw puzzle, the trick is to do the big pieces and edges first, and then fill in the rest with the fiddly bits. Even better than a jigsaw puzzle, if a piece almost fits, you can knock off a bit to make it fit. You'll need a hammer, a chisel, and safety glasses. Mark the cut (straight lines only), then chisel back and forth along the line. Hold the chisel upright, and keep the chisel edge aligned with the mark. Tap gently at first—a heavy hand is likely to break the stone in the wrong direction. As the mark becomes a groove, and the stone figures out where you want it to break, you can bang away a little harder.

8. When the puzzle is complete, sweep more stonedust into the cracks between the pavers. Then use a garden hose to

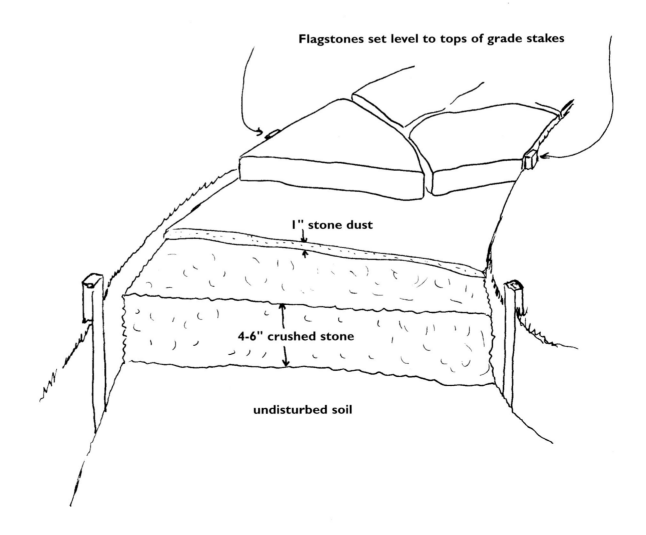

Flagstones set level to tops of grade stakes

1" stone dust

4-6" crushed stone

undisturbed soil

Brush stonedust into the cracks to stabilize the pavers

squirt a hard stream of water into the cracks, washing the filler under the edges of the stones and into any remaining gaps. As you walk the surface and flush the cracks, some stones will settle unevenly. Pry up any low edge with a crowbar, and hold it in position while you flush more stone-dust into the crack. It will take several days of walking on the surface to find all the wobblers and more sweeping and squirting to stabilize them.

9. Rake some of the excavated dirt back up against the edges of the path, and slope it for easy mowing. If you want to keep the grass out of the path, you'll need landscape edging to provide a barrier between the path and the sod. Whatever you do, some plants will eventually sprout in the cracks between the stones. You can mow them, pull them, or turn the invasion into a virtue by planting your own selections first. Portulaca and creeping phlox will bloom in the cracks. Mother-of-thyme spreads in a tough mat that will choke out most weeds and release a delicate scent when walked upon. No summer is long enough for cottagers to wear a rut in flag-stone and mother-of-thyme.

BADMINTON COURT

On a rainy day in the 1860s, the Duke of Beaufort's bored house guests stretched a cord across a hall in the Duke's ancestral home and began knocking a cork and feather shuttlecock over the cord. The game eventually adopted the name of the house, Badminton. Although serious players stay indoors—where the absence of wind removes all excuses—the outdoor version has become a backyard classic.

It's an ideal cottage game: simple rules, no steroids, few injuries, and it requires only 44' of beach or lawn. More to the point, when the cottage budget cringes at the cost of jet skis and docks, consider that a full set of badminton gear costs under $20. That's the good news.

The bad news is that a full set of badminton gear costs under $20. The cheap equipment—flimsy collapsible poles, invisible string guys, and a net that's harder to untangle than a wad of spider web—is guaranteed to collapse under the weight of the morning dew, trip the dog, and drive the poor lawn mower pusher to utter frustration. Now, I appreciate that the Duke of Beaufort's guests might have been more concerned about whacking an ancestral chandelier with an overhand smash than they were with the awkwardness of mowing under the net, but maybe, just maybe, if the badminton set cost as much as Beaufort's chandelier, somebody would remember to put it away at night.

Before you toss out a perfectly good game over the irritating tangle of shoddy gear, try these simple court reforms.

All the pole has to do is hold the net 5' off the ground and get out of the way of the lawn mower. The collapsible feature is there for the convenience of the packager, not the user, not unless you're planning to pack the poles in your suitcase when you go. A sturdy 2 x 2 makes a better post than those cursed tinfoil

A simple wooden box will hold the post upright in shallow soil

tubes and is cheap enough to leave behind at the end of the season. Rip a 2 x 4 in half, or buy 2 x 2s at the lumber yard (where they make 2 x 2s by ripping a 2 x 4 in half).

You could, in theory, sharpen the end of the wooden post and drive it a couple of feet into the ground, so it could stand up straight without the help of strings and stakes. In theory. In practice, the "just drive it into the ground" solution requires that you climb a moderately high ladder before being able to hit the top of an 8' post with the sledge hammer. In practice, there's one big rock just under the grass, which has been waiting there for the last 3 ½ gazillion years for somebody to come along to try and drive a stake in that

Using the cut-off ends of the 2x2 post as sides, or spacers, will ensure a perfect fit.

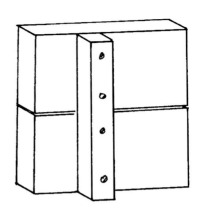

spot (in fact, the only word some rocks know is "gotcha"). And even if you do manage to climb the ladder, hammer the post, and elude the gotcha rock, at the very best you'll have a solid, permanent post...and one more thing to mow around for the rest of the summer.

The answer is to build a better post hole. All you need is a few scraps of lumber and some screws. We used six odd bits of 2 x 6, which, if you put them back together, might make a single board 5-6' long. But use whatever scraps you have at hand. The object is make a simple, skinny box—a socket to hold the end of our 2 x 2 post.

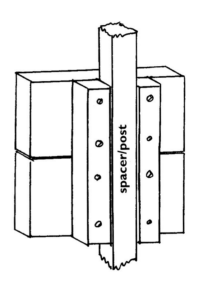

If you ripped your posts from a full-length 2 x 4, you'll have two posts, 96" long. Cut two 11" pieces off each post. You now have two 74" poles and four 11" pieces. The short pieces are spacers, to keep the two faces of each socket exactly one post-thickness apart.

Lay out two 2 x 6 scraps side by side and screw one of the 11" spacers across them. Screw a second spacer parallel to the first and one post-width away (using yet another piece of 2 x 2 to set the first two spacers the right distance apart). The 2 x 2 probably won't be perfectly square, so match the thicknesses

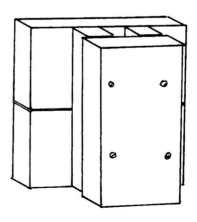

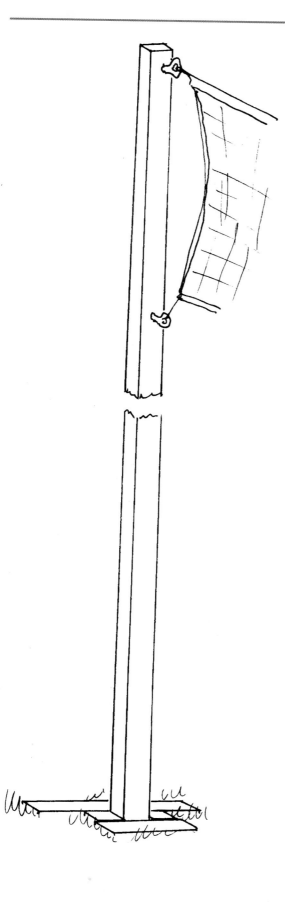

when you lay out the spacers. Just keep in mind that the post has to slide between them.

The two spacers, fastened across the 2 x 6 scraps, form a skinny, three-sided box. Close the fourth side with more scrap. Screw it down. Then make sure the post slides in and out of the socket.

Dig a hole 11" deep, chuck out the gotcha rock, and drop the wooden socket into the hole. Slide the post into its socket, and hold the post in vertical alignment while you fix the socket into position. Kick the socket, or hammer it, to settle it in the dirt at the bottom of the hole.

With the top of the socket flush with the ground, holding the post in the vertical position, tamp the dirt back in around the socket. Tamp it hard, with a hammer if you have to, and replace the sod at the top. That's it. Set the second post the same way but at least 20' away (stretching the net between them will simplify the spacing).

The net is supposed to be 5' high at center court. It will sag a bit, so measure about 62" up the post from ground level, drill a hole, and

With the wooden hole set flush to the sod, it's an easy matter to lift the post and mow over the hole.

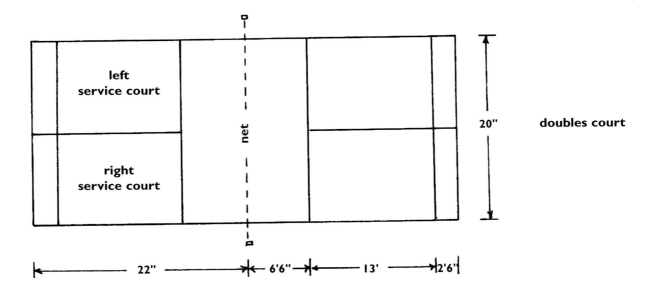

left
service court

net

right
service court

20"   doubles court

|← 22" →|← 6'6" →|← 13' →|2'6'|

attach an eye bolt there to tie the top of the net. Note that if you put the 74" post 11" into the socket, you'll have 63" of post sticking up—one inch more than you need.

Attach the net at the top, then pull down the bottom tie to find the best spot for the bottom eye bolt.

An official doubles court is 44' long and 20' wide. Measuring the lines is easy. The hard part is getting the corners square. If you're expecting guests who quibble over such things, use a string to lay the court out geometrically as follows:

1. Set two little stakes, 20' apart (17' for a singles court), under the net.

2. Tie a loop at one end of the string and slip it over a stake.

3. Stretch out the string, measure off 22' from the stake, and tie a knot.

4. Measure off another 29' 8 ¾" (27' 9 ⅝" for singles) and tie another loop.

5. Put the second loop over the second stake.

6. Grasp the knot and back away from the net until both sides of the string are taut.

7. The string forms a triangle with the net as the base and the knot at one back corner of the court. Mark it.

8. Switch the loops from one stake to the other and pull the string taut again to find the other back corner of the court. Mark it.

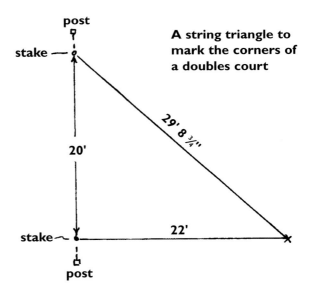

post

stake

A string triangle to mark the corners of a doubles court

29' 8 ¾"

20'

stake

22'

post

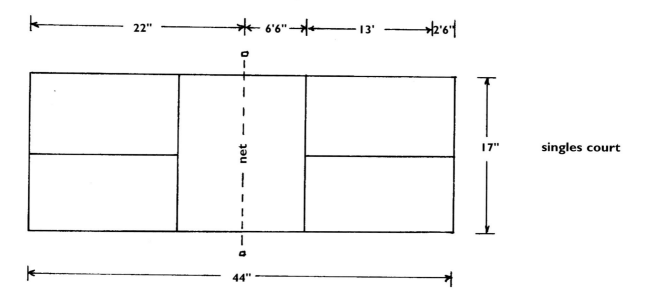

22" | 6'6" | 13' | 2'6"

net

17"   singles court

44"

RULES

The server begins from the right-hand service court, serving diagonally across the net into the opponents' service court. Underhand serves only, please; save the overhand smash for the rally.

Unlike tennis, only one serve attempt is allowed. If the shuttlecock hits the top of the net and still falls into the opponents' service court, it's a valid serve, not a "let" as in tennis.

After the serve, the rally continues until one side fails to return the shuttlecock over the net into the opponents' court.

Only the server can score. In singles play, if the server wins the rally, he delivers the second serve from his left-hand service court, alternating courts with each point. If the opponent wins the rally, service changes sides and no points are scored.

In the doubles game, each partner serves in turn.

Play continues to 15 or 21. And remember to change ends with each game to give your opponents equal access to the wind and sun-in-the-eyes excuses.

9. The two corner marks should be exactly 20' apart.

10. Repeat the procedure on the opposite side of the net, using the original stakes under the net.

Now you can stretch the string from corner to corner and use it as a guide to mark all the outside boundaries. Using whitewash and a brush, paint the lines right on the grass. If whitewash is hard to find, buy a bag of lime at the garden store and trickle it along the lines. In small quantities, neither whitewash nor lime will harm the grass. Either will last for weeks. You can reapply the lines as they fade. Better still, you can mow right over them.

The breakthrough, however, is at the net. You can lift out this post with one hand, push the mower right over the socket, replace the post, and carry on with barely a break in stride. No invisible guy strings to trip wanderers in the dark. No collapsing poles. And no more conflict between those who play and those who maintain the court.

FIREWOOD STORAGE

Cross braces at the bottom tie the front frame to the back.

MATERIALS

2 x 4 studs
10' long
6 pieces

1 x 6 board
8' long
1 piece

½" plywood
2 x 8' (half sheet)
1 piece

¼" bolts
3 ½" long
8

 # 8 screws
3" long
20

shakes or shingles
1 bundle

shingle nails

Everybody knows that firewood should be dry. Wet wood sizzles and smokes and leaves a goo of flammable creosote up the flue. So, if firewood has to be dried, why not pile it out of sight to season awhile? Throw a sheet of plastic over it to keep off the rain?

Why not? Because both of those common mistakes overlook the fact that a lot of water came with the wood. Up to half the weight of freshly cut wood is water—sap trapped in the tree when it was cut. Piling it out of sight usually means a damp, shady nook behind the cottage, protected from the breeze. And while a waterproof cover might shed the rain, it also traps the original moisture in, like a load of wet laundry sealed in a green plastic garbage bag.

The best way to season firewood is to split it and then stack it out in the open, where sunshine and dry summer breezes can draw the moisture out of the wood...much like drying laundry.

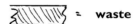 = waste

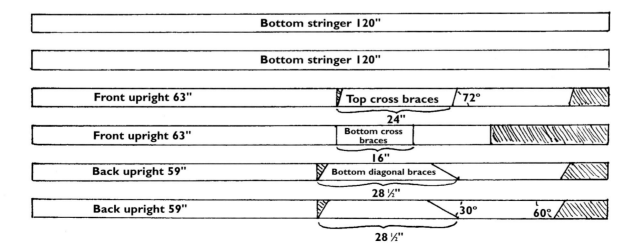

Common sense still insists on something to keep off the rain. And our tidy genes suggest that if the pile is to be out in the open for sun and wind and all to see, then it will have to be kept in neater order than that jumble behind the shed.

All of which leads to this lightweight firewood storage rack. It's one row wide to let the wind get through to do its work. It sports two bottom stringers to keep the wood up off the damp ground. It has a simple roof

**Diagonal braces will keep
the two ends upright.**

to shed rain without blocking the wind. And it's designed to hold one face cord of fuel—a handy measure if you want to double-check the supplier's word on whether that really was a full face cord in the back of his truck.

This structure is so simple that you don't need a building inspector. Start with the bottom stringers, then uprights at each end to hold the firewood, and diagonals to brace it square. The roof is an option. Stacking the firewood bark-side up does almost as much as a roof to shed the rain.

Cut the 2 x 4s to length as shown in the plans. The angled cuts for the two top cross braces are roughly 72°. There's nothing special about 72°, but it will be a little simpler if all the angles match. Cut the angles on a table saw or a miter saw. Or use a jig like the one shown for the picnic table project.

The bottom diagonal braces are cut 60° on one end and 30° on the other. Again, use a table saw, miter saw, or jig to cut matching angles on these four bottom braces.

1. Lay out a 10' bottom stringer and mark the positions for the two front uprights, which are 84" apart or 18" from either end of the stringer.

2. Overlap a 63" upright outside the mark and drill a ¼" bolt hole through the stringer and upright.

3. Bolt the stringer and upright together, with the nut on the upright side.

4. Screw the diagonal bottom brace to the outside edge of the upright, with the tip of the sharply angled end 25" up the side of the upright; predrill the screw hole.

5. Use a square to make sure that the stringer and the upright are perpendicular to one another.

6. Then drill and bolt the free end of the brace to the end of the stringer.

7. Repeat steps 1-6 on the opposite end of the stringer, bolting and bracing the other 63" front upright.

8. Repeat steps 1-7 with the second stringer, using the shorter 59" back uprights.

You now have two halves of the rack: a front assembly (with the taller uprights) and a back assembly (with the shorter uprights).

Stand the two assemblies side by side, with the uprights on the inside and about a foot apart. Join the two assemblies with the 16" cross braces at the bottom. If you set the ends of each cross brace flush with the outer faces of the stringers, you'll get the spacing right. If you set the braces perpendicular to the stringers and check them with the square, you'll square the whole assembly. Fasten the braces with two screws at each end.

It stands, but the four uprights are free at the top and floppy. Attach the two top braces. Keep the tops of the front and back uprights a foot apart, and set the top edge of each brace flush with the tops of the uprights. Drive one screw through the brace and into

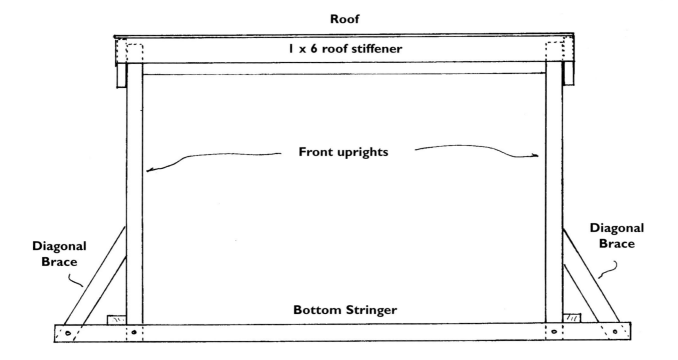

Roof

I x 6 roof stiffener

Front uprights

Diagonal Brace

Diagonal Brace

Bottom Stringer

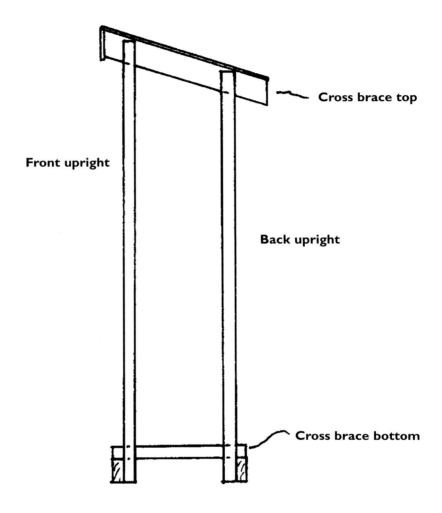

Cross brace top

Front upright

Back upright

Cross brace bottom

the taller upright; another screw into the shorter upright. Check to ensure that both uprights are vertical, then reinforce the brace with two more screws.

The two top braces also serve as rafters to hold the roof. The last structural piece, the long 1 x 6, can be nailed to the front of the rafters, nailed to the back of the rafters, or fit-ted in between them. It isn't there to brace the ends so much as to stiffen the roof. If you're expecting a heavy snow load, you might want two longitudinal stiffeners—one in the front like this one and another at the back—to keep the roof from sagging.

The roof can be just about anything. We used a piece of plywood because it happened to be lying around. Boards would do the job. So would a piece of roofing steel.

Unlike roofing steel, our plywood roof will need waterproofing to survive the winter. We nailed on shakes. But a roll of roofing paper, or some leftover shingles, would serve the purpose as well.

Adding further weather protection around the back or the sides would not be an improvement. Yes, rain can blow into this rack, but the wood will dry faster if you let the wind blow through, rain or shine.

Emptied, this rack is still light enough to carry around. You can move it up on the verandah for the autumn fireplace season or hide it out behind the cottage when you don't need it. But during the summer, when it's supposed to be drying firewood, keep it out in the open in the breeze. Your fires will crackle instead of fizz.

Cover the top if you must, but leave the sides of any firewood pile open to the breeze.

TIMBER
STEPS

MATERIALS

6 x 6 timber

　(pressure-treated)

　10' long

　1 per step

spikes

　8" long

　6 per step

crushed rock

　¾" clear

　approximately 1 ton

surface material of choice:

　stonedust

　wood chips

　flagstones

　interlocking pavers

The crushed rock will be cheap at the quarry but expensive to haul. If you have access to a pickup or trailer, haul your own. If you have to have it delivered, you might as well get a whole dump truck load and use the extra to fix the cottage road, share with the neighbors, or use on another project, like the flagstone path.

Right after death and taxes is the sure bet that the cottage is uphill from the lake. If the hill is too steep for easy walking, some steps may be in order.

How steep is too steep for walking? That might depend on whether you're six or sixty. But in some jurisdictions it's also answered in the building code. In general, an 8% slope is considered to be the maximum for paths or ramps.

Slope, as a percentage, is the rise (vertical) divided by the run (horizontal). So if the cottage is 7' higher than the lake and 100' away from the water's edge, the slope over that whole distance would be 7%. That would be an easily walked path if the slope were constant. In the real world, however, little is constant.

At my friend Doug's, where we built these stairs, there's a sharp 2' rise from the relatively flat lower lawn to the leveled fill around the cottage. That's a 2' rise in about a 5' run, or a 40% slope over this little stretch! That calls for some steps.

And the first step is to excavate 6-8" deep at the bottom and into the face of the slope, where the steps will go, removing any roots

rise/run = slope

rise

run

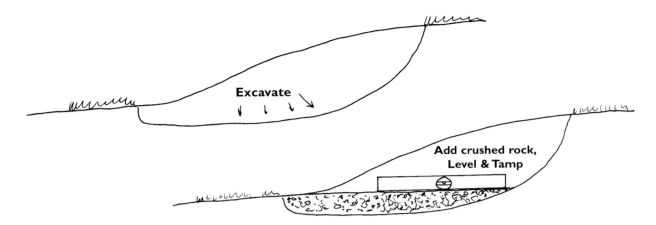

Excavate

Add crushed rock,
Level & Tamp

or soft organic soil that would allow the steps to shift. Fill the bottom of the hole with crushed rock, rake it level, and tamp it down with a lawn roller or plate compactor. The crushed rock is for drainage, combating both frost heaves and erosion. And it provides a solid, unsinkable base.

Deciding just how many steps takes a little calculation. First, accept that every step must be the same height. If we have to ascend 24" and want to use 7" steps, we cannot have three 7" steps and one 3" step. That would guarantee stumbles, trips, and spilled drinks. The path can slope, but the steps must all be the same height. If it doesn't come out even, alter the slope of the path a little. Here, for instance, we decided to use 6 x 6 timbers (actually 5 ½ x 5 ½") as steps. If each timber gives a rise of 5 ½", four steps will get us up 22". In need of another 2" of

For safety and comfort, every step must be the same height.

rise, we added a bit more crushed rock at the bottom, raising that end of the path an inch. And we raked down the dirt above the steps to lower that part of the path an inch. Now the difference between the two paths is 22", exactly the height of our four steps.

The other secret to stumble-free steps is to fit them to a natural stride. We take longer strides climbing low steps, and we shorten our stride when climbing higher steps. Your local building code will spell out the limits precisely, but as a rule of thumb multiply the rise times the run (the height of each step times the distance between them). The product, in inches, should be somewhere between 70 and 75. So, these timber steps should be at least 13" apart (5 ½" x 13" = 71.5").

Timber steps aren't the only choice. Brick and concrete are common, and big flat stones are a natural in cottage country. But

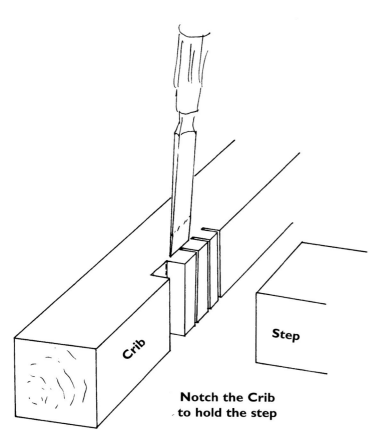

Notch the Crib to hold the step

the rules on rise and run are the same no matter what material you use. Design has a freer hand when choosing the width of the steps. A 2-3' width is sufficient for a single stroller, but allow twice that much for side-by-side walks.

Side by side or one at a time, walkers put all their weight on the outside edge of a step. And there's fill behind that step, pushing it forward. If it isn't properly locked in place, the step will try to roll downhill. With timber, we can lock each step into position by fitting the ends into crib timbers at the sides. From a 10' timber, we can cut one 54" step and two 33" cribs. A 33" crib is just long enough to cover the notch in the crib below and support the ends of the step above.

To notch the crib, set the circular saw at a 1 ½" depth, and make a series of parallel cuts, or kerfs, in the notch area. Then remove the waste between the cuts with a chisel. Fit the notch around the end of the step and tighten it up with an 8" spike.

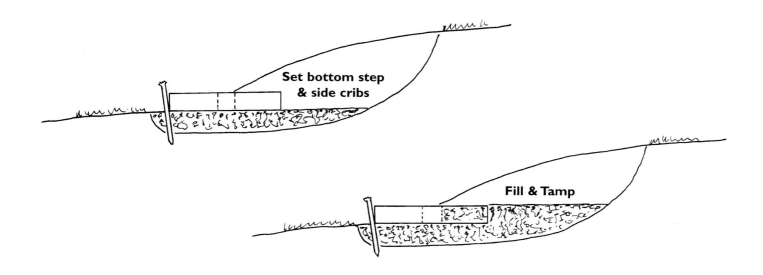

Set bottom step & side cribs

Fill & Tamp

With a crib spiked to each end, you've made a letter H. Set the H on the crushed rock base and level it carefully. Every subsequent step will rest on the one below, so if you start crooked it will be hard to correct. Level the first H, even if it means reraking the surface of the crushed rock base. When everything is level, drive in stakes on either side of the first H and a couple in front of it, to keep it from being dislodged when you build the subsequent steps above it.

Fill in behind the step with more crushed rock; level and compact the fill. You won't eas-

A notched crib at each end locks the step in place so that it can't roll down the hill.

ily fit a plate compactor or lawn roller behind the step, so tamp the crushed rock hard with one of the cut-off timbers. The more you tamp now, the less settling will occur later. Brush any loose grit off the top of the step and add another H. Set each new step 13-14" back from the last one, and spike the sides to the crib below. The spikes keep the

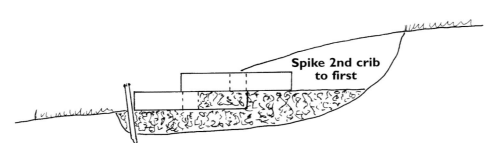

Spike 2nd crib to first

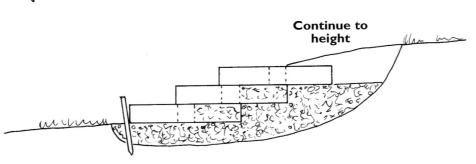

Continue to height

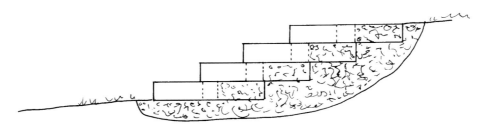

step from pushing forward when you compact the new fill behind it. If you don't have a heavy hammer to drive the spikes, drill a hole in the top timber to start the spike.

Restore slope

Compacted crushed rock makes a stable surface, especially if you top it off with some stonedust. But it isn't the fanciest surface, and it may not match the path. For a different look, partially fill behind the step with compacted crushed rock, leaving just enough room for flagstones, pavers, bricks, pea gravel, or wood chips. You still need the crushed

rock underneath for drainage and stability, but you can cap it with whatever looks right and feels comfy enough for bare feet. Whatever you use, the top surface of the finish paving material should come up flush with the top of the timber step.

The rest is landscaping: Remove the stakes in front of the bottom step, back fill and contour the slope outside the cribs, and finish the path to the top and bottom of the steps.

If you have more than three or four steps, there is one final consideration: handrails. Your local building code might even require them on longer flights of outdoor steps. The alternative to handrails is to build a series of smaller flights, like this one, with three or four steps, then a landing, a turning, or a terrace.

Each step assembly looks like a letter H. Lay it flat, fill in behind, and add the next one.

SUNDIAL

This equatorial sundial is merely a model of the globe...without the globe. The gnomon—in this case the narrow rod that casts the shadow—represents the axis of the earth. The hour curve, where the numbers are marked, is the equator. If you tip the gnomon to the exact latitude of your cottage and point the axis due north, the sun will strike the model just as it strikes the earth. As a final step, we'll make some minor adjustments to match solar time to the clock.

There are four essential pieces: the base, the stand, the equator, and the gnomon. We used a ⅛" steel rod from the hobby shop as our gnomon. It's sold as piano rod. Steel is not the ideal material, however. It rusts and will distract the compass used to point the gnomon north. A brass rod would be better but may be harder to find, and a little more expensive.

An equatorial sundial mimics the earth. Earth's axis is the gnomon, and its shadow marks the hours around the equator.

The base, stand, and equator can be cut from wood. We used a 1 x 12" pine board. You could substitute plywood, but any wood will weather. If you want your wooden sundial to last more than a summer, you will have to seal it carefully with exterior varnish, paint, urethane, or tung oil.

First, the equator. Trace two semicircles with a compass, using a common center and placing the outer arc at least 1 ½" beyond the inner arc. Use a protractor to divide the equator into 12 equal parts by marking the equator every 15°. These marks will become the hour lines.

Cut out the equator piece

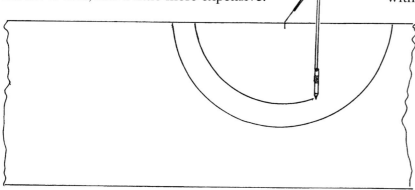

Trace two semicircles with a compass, using a common center.

Divide the equator into 12 equal parts by marking the equator every 15°

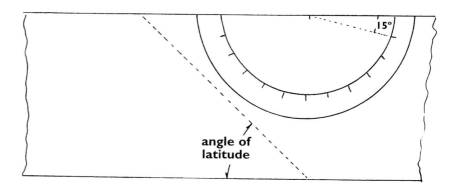

15°

angle of latitude

with a jigsaw, bandsaw, or coping saw. Sand the saw cuts carefully to finish precisely at the semicircular lines. Now use a square to extend the hour lines across the inner surface—the concave curve of the equator piece.

Now the stand. Select the straightest, squarest edge of the board to be the bottom. Find the exact latitude of the cottage from a detailed topographical map. Then mark the angle of latitude from the bottom edge of the board, using a protractor. This angle is the critical part of the design. Don't copy the angle from these drawings or from another sundial. Use the angle of your own latitude. This line shows where the gnomon will go.

Place the point of the compass on this line and draw an arc with the same diameter as the equator piece. Or use the equator piece itself to trace the curve. The inner curve of the stand is exactly the same diameter as the inner curve of the equator piece. When you eventually cut the curve, leave an extra inch

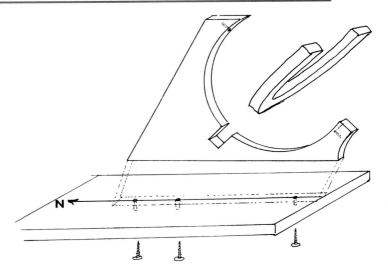

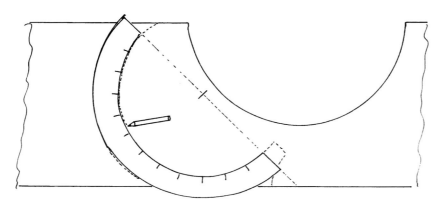

The inner curve of the stand is exactly the same diameter as the inner curve of the equator piece.

or so of arc beyond the straight line intersection, so the curve is a little longer than a semicircle. You'll need that excess later to hold the gnomon.

Cut out the stand just as you cut out the equator piece. Add a notch halfway around the semicircle to hold the equator. The size of the notch depends on the width and thickness of the equator piece. Mark it closely for a snug fit. Drill holes for the gnomon rod at the two points where the axis crosses the semicircle.

The base is the least critical piece. Draw a center line and screw the stand to the base from underneath. If the stand straddles the center line and the center line is turned north-south, then the dial is easily aligned.

Mount the base on any solid, level surface. A rock, stump, or deck railing will do. The dial must be mounted so that the gnomon points due north. You can use a good compass, adjusting for the difference between magnetic north and true north with the correction shown

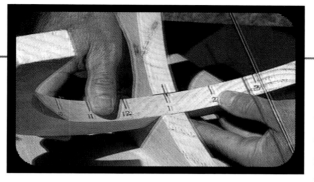

on your topographical map. Or you can align the gnomon with the North Star.

Finally, level the base. If the mounting surface isn't level, use shims under the corners

In summer, we have to adjust our markers one hour for Daylight Savings Time; and we have to adjust for the fact that we're not in the exact center of our hour-wide time zone.

of the base or leveling screws. Check with a spirit level or a saucer of water.

Slide the equator piece into the notch for final adjustments. In theory, at high noon the gnomon's shadow should fall straight along the center of the stand and should cross the equator piece at the halfway mark, the one we marked at 90° around the semicircle. In theory. In fact, your cottage is probably not precisely in the center of your time zone, and the sun will get there sooner or later than the clock says it should. And it will be at least another hour off if you've moved to daylight saving time.

The adjustment is simple. If the dial is level, points due north, and if the gnomon's angle matches your latitude, the adjustment for longitude and daylight saving time is to simply move the equatorial piece around until solar time matches the clock. You can fasten it there with a screw if you like.

There will be days when it appears that the sundial is running slow or fast. In fact, it's probably quite accurate. No need to alarm the children, but the earth's orbit is not a tidy circle. The planet speeds up, slows down, and wobbles on its axis enough to throw solar time out of kilter by a quarter of an hour or more some days. Our little wooden timepiece will measure the passage of the sun quite accurately. Any discrepancy between the sundial and your earth clock can be blamed on the idiosyncrasies of solar time, not on flaws of workmanship.

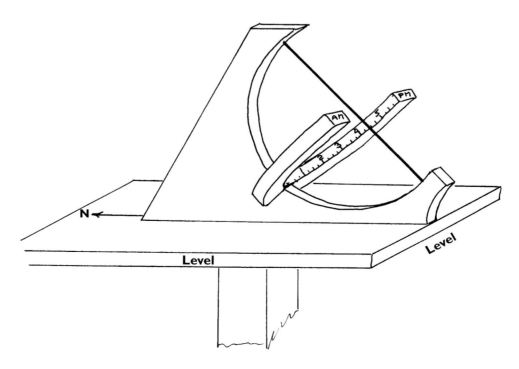

PAINTS
AND
STAINS

Any wood left outdoors is going to suffer over time. Not just wear and tear. Sunlight and ultraviolet damage, dry winds that can lead to checking and cracking, damp weather that encourages fungus and rot—everything takes its toll. Even naturally weather-resistant wood like cedar will eventually discolor and crack.

We know what the problems are, but the marketplace offers such a bewildering array of solutions and competing claims that selecting just the right wood protection becomes a chore in itself.

First, an overview. Most of that confusion in the outdoor paint department can be divided into three broad categories: paint, stain, and preservatives. In a nutshell, "paint" seals wood at the surface, while "stain" soaks through the surface and seals within the top layer of wood. Both paint and stain preserve wood to the extent that they succeed in sealing the weather out. But plain "preservatives" take a chemical approach to kill fungi, mildew, and other organic beasties that would otherwise feast on the unprotected wood.

Okay, okay, my three broad categories omit a gazillion trade name choices invoking euphemisms like shield, screen, system this, and poly-something that. Not to mention the more familiar varnish, urethane, and oil finishes. The trade name solutions provide excellent protection, but the point here is to sort through the confusion, not to rate the brands. Understand that no matter what they call the stuff, it still protects wood by sealing out the weather and stopping organic decay. Even if the salesperson calls it "Saint Miracle's Eternal Life Atomic Umbrella," you must still remember to ask: "Does this stuff seal like paint, penetrate like stain, or preserve with bug killer?"

Varnish and oil finishes have been around for too long to dismiss without comment. Varnish, and its latter-day urethane successors, form hard, durable skins. But outdoor wood is subject to cycles of wet and dry, hot and cold, which cause the wood to expand and contract. Put a rigid varnish skin on moving wood, and the skin is going to crack and peel. Which is why varnish and its successors need annual maintenance. Penetrating oil finishes don't crack, but neither do they protect wood against UV discoloration. And the oil, itself, will dry out and need regular reapplications.

Stain one section at a time to maintain a wet edge.

So, let's get back to plain terms like paint, stain, and preservatives. Then weigh the choices against some real-life applications.

Take something like a cottage chair, for example. If you like the look of natural wood, you might consider using a clear finish. That lets all the beauty of the wood show through. But it also lets the sunshine get through to the wood, and sunshine—with its ultraviolet rays—will soon turn the surface grey. Clear preservatives and water repellents, like stain, soak into the surface. The very clarity, however, leaves the surface open to UV damage.

Semitransparent stains are a compromise. They contain enough blocking agents to limit UV exposure and slow the aging process, but

Semi-transparent stains provide some protection without completely hiding the wood's natural look.

they also block some of the natural look.

Semitransparent stains won't be tough enough for wear-and-tear areas like the deck or the picnic table. There we'll need the addi-

STAINS

New wood often has a "mill glaze" on the surface, a smooth finish with a faint shine. That glaze will prevent optimum penetration of the stain. Fill the screw holes, sand everything, and then let new wood weather for a few weeks—just to open up the surface pores to help the stain sink in. Then sand it again just before staining. Use #80 to #120 grit sandpaper, sand with the grain, and clean up the dust before staining.

Choose a warm, dry day, and avoid direct sunlight if possible. Stir the can thoroughly, and stir it again every 15 minutes as you work.

Brush the stain on generously and quickly, working along the grain and keeping a wet edge. If the piece is composed of separate boards (like a cottage chair), complete one board at a time to avoid leaving a dry edge, which will darken when you come back and overlap it.

After 15 minutes, go back over the surface with a dry cloth, wiping off any excess stain. This might require doing larger pieces in stages, stopping to wipe and stir every 15 minutes, for example. If you don't wipe it off, any liquid that hasn't soaked into the wood may start to dry on the surface, leaving a gummy, uneven finish.

tional protection of an opaque stain. As stains, they're designed to penetrate the surface. The opacity provides maximum UV blockage and opens the way for a wide variety of colors.

In opaque stains, the basic choice is between latex-based products and oil-based or alkyd stains. Latex finishes are easier to apply—you can clean the drips and brushes with water—but they do powder. Not only will the surface wear away with traffic, but color will soon be tracked off the deck and into the cottage. Leave the latex finishes for the siding and other look-but-don't-touch applications. For the deck, pick an alkyd stain or something that says it is made specifically for decks. For furniture, like the picnic table, alkyd products will provide more resistance to grease and food stains.

Opaque stains are applied much like other stains, with one critical difference at the end. Sand the wood, stir the can, brush on the stain, and keep a wet edge, but don't wipe it off at the end! Wiping will smear the color into one almighty mess.

PAINTS

If you're going to hide the natural wood with canned pigments, it's not much of a step up to a tough exterior paint. Paint does have to be reapplied periodically, but a good paint job will last for years. Again, the big choice is between latex and oil-based or alkyd

Rough, old paint can be softened with a heat gun or scraped off, or...

simply sanded smooth.

PAINTS

Fill the screw holes and sand everything with #80 to #120 grit sandpaper. Sand with the grain, and clean up the dust before painting. Prime any raw wood, especially new wood, and let the prime coat dry.

Choose a warm, dry day, and avoid direct sunlight if possible. Stir the can thoroughly, and stir it again every 15 minutes as you work.

Apply the paint with a brush, a roller, or a sponge applicator. And don't be too generous with the paint. If you try to apply it too thickly, it will run. If the first coat doesn't cover satisfactorily, just let it dry and then apply a second coat.

paints. And the same criteria apply: Choose latex for convenience or alkyd for durability.

Do remember, however, that key distinction between paints and stains. Stains penetrate the surface; paints cover the surface. For stain, we prepared the wood by sanding it raw—no old finishes, not even the mill glaze—all in the interest of penetration. Now, with paint, we actually want to limit the penetration and keep the paint on the surface. If the paint soaks into the wood it can look blotchy.

The bad news is that any raw wood, especially new wood, should be primed. You can buy special "primer" or, alternatively, thin some ordinary paint to prepare the raw wood. Thinning encourages penetration. The primer penetrates, dries, and seals much like a stain (only uglier). The good paint that goes on top of the primer stays at the surface where it belongs, doesn't penetrate, and doesn't go blotchy.

If priming is the bad news, the good news is that paint covers a lot of surface faults that stain would reveal—like the remains of the old finish, impenetrable knots, or wood filler. All that's required is that you reduce the old finish to a smooth surface. You can scrape off the old peeling paint, sand it, or melt it off with a heat gun. If you leave some old color behind, no matter. Just get it smooth, and seal any raw spots with primer.

PRESERVATIVE

Here's where faith and knowledge go their separate ways. Faith in the commercial claims would have us believe that chemistry can do miracles. Knowing what's in the can suggests the miracles might be limited. For simplicity's sake, let's divide all that canned chemistry into waterproofing, fungicides, pretreated wood, and old-fashioned creosote.

Waterproofing, sometimes called sealant, sheds water if properly and regularly applied. It does not prevent UV discoloration, and it does not completely prevent the drying, checking, and cracking caused by the weather. It is a supplement, not a substitute for paint or stain.

The hard-core preservatives kill the beasties of mold, fungus, and mildew with fungicides. Some of these preservatives are colored, some clear. They can provide some protection against rot, and the colored ones (like green copper napthenate) can partially block UV rays. They do not, however, stop the drying, checking, and cracking. And anything potent enough to kill fungus might not be entirely healthy for humans.

Pretreated or pressure-treated wood has become a common feature in do-it-yourself building. It saves you the mess (and presumed risk) of applying liquid fungicides yourself. You still wouldn't want to lick the deck, however. And pressure-treated wood is still sub-ject to drying, checking, and cracking.

Most of the preservatives described above can be used in conjunction with paint. Old-fashioned creosote, however, not only colors the wood a permanent, oily black, it also bleeds into anything adjacent to the treated piece. It is still an effective preservative, but save it for underground applications, like the buried end of a post, for example.

Picking the right protection for outdoor wood means more than just choosing the color. It helps to know which kind of stuff does what. But don't hesitate to ask for specific advice in the paint department, and get exactly what you need to keep the weather away from your wood.

EAVES TROUGH
AND
RAINBARREL

Fixing up the eaves trough is one of those chores that usually comes to mind on a rainy day, but it is easier to do when it's dry.

The problem is that the roof collects 1,000 square feet or more of rain and then dumps it all at the eaves. In some places, that doesn't much matter. But if that falling curtain of runoff is washing out the flowerbeds, splattering the siding, or eroding the lawn into little ravines, you've got a problem. If it's also running down the back of your neck every time you step out the door—which happens to be the case here—you've got a problem and a personal incentive to solve it.

PLANNING AND PREPARATION

Old eaves trough installations deteriorate in time. Heavy snow, falling ice, and clunky ladders sooner or later lead to a case of the leaky sags. If it's merely showing its age, you can use the original installation as a guide to how many bits and pieces you'll need and where the downspouts go.

If you're starting from scratch, draw a sketch of the roof as if you were looking down on it from above. Record the measurements along the eaves. The sketch is your planning guide, and the first step is to decide where the downspouts will go. You'll want at least one downspout for every 40' of gutter. If you have too few downspouts, they won't be able to handle a heavy rain and the gutters will overflow—which rather defeats the purpose. Mark downspout locations in places where they won't interfere with windows, doors, or walkways. And, if the downspout is intended to simply dump the runoff onto the ground, plan locations with natural drainage in mind; it's no good diverting rain off the roof and onto a slope where it will immediately run back into the basement.

When you've located a downspout, that will be the low point of any run. The high point will be at the opposite end of the run. Divide any long, straight gutter runs into 10' sections (the standard length of a pre-fabricated gutter). From the sketch, you can now count the number of connectors, end caps, inside corners, and outside corners the installation will require.

While you're measuring the roof, have a close look at the condition of the fascia and of the drip edge.

Mark the fascia with a chalkline, sloped at least ⅛" for every 10' of gutter.

This simple dove tail hanger makes installation a snap.

The fascia (pronounced "facer" in some areas) is that board which covers the ends of the rafters at the eaves, and it's the board to which we fasten the eaves trough. It is often the first piece of the roof to rot and is easily replaced—if you do it now, before the eaves trough goes on.

The drip edge is just what it sounds like— a slight projection of flashing or shingle at the roof edge, above the fascia. It's intended to let the water drip freely rather than run down the fascia board. A metal roof, or asphalt shingles with metal along the eaves, is probably doing an adequate job. Older asphalt shingles, however, can bend, flop, and fail at the projection. If that's the case, add some metal or vinyl drip edge to your shopping list.

The planning, to this point, is the same for all types of do-it-yourself eaves troughs. Now you have to decide between metal and vinyl and several different design styles. Here, we installed a vinyl system with a traditional look. The details differ, but the elements of installation are common to all sys-

tems: Maintain the slope from high point to low point, seal the connections, and don't fall off the ladder.

INSTALLATION

Don't assume that the eaves are level. Start at the high end of each gutter run and drive a small nail about ½" from the top of the fascia. Stretch a chalk line from the nail to the opposite end of the gutter run (where the downspout will go). Level the chalk line with a line level or a carpenter's level, then snap the chalk line on the fascia. That's level. The bubble says so.

The manufacturer of this particular system says the water will run downhill if we lower one end by ⅛" for every 10' of gutter. On this 30' gutter run, that would be ⅜". I have to believe, however, that the manufacturer had a keen eye on the bubble and a steady hand on the chalk line. I was concentrating on not falling off the ladder, and I knew that I might not have been quite so precise in snapping the level line to such tight tolerances. So, I dropped the low end more than recommended. The water will still run downhill, only faster.

Anyway, lower the end of the chalk line at the downspout location and snap a second line. This second line, the guide line, is sloped from the high end to the downspout. We'll use the guide line to attach the hangers.

These dovetail hangers simply screw into the fascia every 2'. To install a traditional galvanized gutter, we would have to align the gutter itself with the guide line, then drive long nails through from the front lip of the gutter.

These hangers are not only easier to align, they also allow much of the assembly to take place on the ground. We can snap an end cap onto a length of gutter, slide the hooks on from the other end, and pass the assembly up to the top of the ladder. Topside, we'll slide each hook back and forth to align it with its hanger and then just snap it into place.

When the second 10' gutter section is in place, we'll join it to the first. This model uses a two-piece joiner, with two compressible sealing beads on the inside piece. Make sure the contact areas are absolutely clean, then snap in the inner section—centered on the joint.

The other joiner piece fits outside the gut-

ter. It, too, snaps into position and should be centered on the joint. It's a tight fit—and necessarily so—to compress the sealing beads inside. The two gutter sections are now joined together in a (we hope) leakproof union. Together, they should still be able to slide back and forth on the hooks.

Vinyl expands in the heat. Which is why the gutters have to be free to move, and why vinyl systems are designed to let the gutters slide back and forth within the drop outlet. These drop outlets are marked with temperature reference lines. Check the day's temperature, then hold the drop outlet in position and measure from the appropriate temperature line to determine the length of the last gutter piece.

Cutting gutters to length is a hacksaw job. It wobbles and shrieks, but it works. If you're cutting near the end of a length, you can slip on an end cap temporarily, to help stabilize

This vinyl gutter uses a two-piece joiner. The inside piece has two beads of sealant; the outside piece squishes it all together.

the wobbles. Mark the cut with a square. And, if you're cutting metal gutters, wear protective gloves.

With the drop outlet secure, temporarily attach a length of downspout to the wall, where it will ultimately connect to the drop outlet. Place one elbow connector on the top end of the downspout and another elbow beneath the drop outlet. The elbows are directional and may be marked with arrows to show which way the water should flow. They fit into (or over) the other pieces, with some overlap. Push them into position, line up the two elbows, and measure the distance between them. That distance (plus some overlap for each elbow) is the length of downspout needed to make the connection.

ROLL OUT THE BARREL

At the bottom of the downspout, we need some means of diverting the water away from the foundation. An elbow and another length of downspout across the lawn is the simplest, but least satisfactory solution. It gets in the way of the lawn mower and does little more than move the erosion problem 10' farther away from the foundation. You can buy a soft plastic spout that rolls up out of the lawn mower's way or a hinged "diverter" elbow, which pivots up out of the lawn mower's way.

The elegant solution is also the traditional one. The old-fashioned or, in this case, new-fashioned rainbarrel does more than prop up the downspout. It saves water that would otherwise have to be pumped, pressurized, and probably softened before you could wash your hair or water the flowers.

The top outlets allow you to connect several of these rainbarrels in a series, to store as much water as you want. The bottom outlet sports a hose and shutoff valve so you can fill the watering can, the wading pool, or whatever.

With a little planning, you can divert the rain just about anywhere you want it. It will still fall on the weekend, but not down the back of your neck.

A sliding joint at the drop outlet allows vinyl gutters to expand without buckling.

Drain the downspout away from the foundation. Or, into a rainbarrel so it can be re-used.

CHIMNEY CLEANING

Most cottages enjoy some kind of wood burner. If not for cooking, then at least a fireplace to take the chill off a rainy day. And, if I may turn an old cliché—where there's fire there's smoke.

The problem is that wood smoke can leave flammable creosote in the chimney. If the firewood is damp, or not well-seasoned, it leaves more creosote. If the fires are small, cool, or intermittent—as most summer fires are—more creosote. As ironic as it might seem, an occasional summer fire can leave more gunky creosote in the flue than a winter's worth of serious woodburning. And when creosote ignites, you've got a dangerous chimney fire.

No cottage is close enough to a fire station to take a chance like that. Inspect the chimney when you open the cottage, and then periodically throughout the summer.

Where you look depends on how the chimney was built. Most builders will have included a "clean-out" door somewhere. If so, you're in luck; you can inspect the chimney without climbing on the roof.

A masonry chimney (brick, block, or stone) should have a little metal door or removable hatch near ground level, usually on the outside but occasionally in a basement or crawlspace. Lift off the door and step back. If this is your first encounter with the clean-out, you'll be met

Creosote condenses in the flue, setting the stage for a dangerous chimney fire.

with a cascade of soot and ashes. Shovel out the mess and wait a few minutes for the dust to settle. Then reach inside with a hand-held mirror. A purse-sized compact will do in a pinch. Reach right to the back of the clean-out space, under the open flue. Angle the mirror so you can look into the clean-out and up the inside of the chimney. On a clear day, you should be able to see a patch of daylight above—and any guck up the insides of the flue. If you can't see daylight, you've either got a serious cleaning job to do, or there's a rain cap on top of the chimney.

A metal chimney might include a capped elbow, where the vertical turns horizontal to find the woodstove. The stubby bottom bit is closed with a metal cap. Hold a bucket under the stub, remove the metal cap, and—when the dust clears—look straight up the open pipe. Safety goggles will keep any falling grit out of your eyes, and a flashlight will help you see what has to be cleaned.

Some metal stovepipes join a masonry chimney inside the cottage. You can pull the stovepipe out of the

An outside "clean-out" door simplifies soot removal, but do wear a mask.

wall to inspect the masonry flue or use the outside clean-out. The outside inspection makes less mess in the cottage. Either way you'll need a mirror to reach in and look up the flue.

The hardest arrangement to inspect is a fireplace with no clean-out door in the chimney. Unless you can fit two mirrors and an arm inside the fireplace, up through the damper, across the smoke shelf, and under the flue, you're out of luck inspecting from terra firma. You'll have to do it from the roof.

A rooftop inspection is easier in one respect—any dislodged grit will fall the other way instead of in your face. But the added difficulty of getting up there safely (see sidebar) might lead to less frequent inspections. Fall off the roof or burn the place down? A cottager's life is full of choices.

Remove the rain cap and look down the flue. If it's too dark to see, bring a flashlight or a mirror. The mirror reflects sunlight down the darkest hole, a trick I learned while trying to fish a fallen pipe out of the well.

Working on the roof adds a new set of risks.

Use a ladder long enough to extend well above the eaves. Fasten the top of the ladder at the eaves so it can't slide sideways. And, if possible, have a helper to steady the ladder at the bottom.

Choose footwear with the best possible grip. Just this once, forget the safety boots and wear your sneakers. Even with sneakers, walking on shingles will damage them if they're cold enough to be brittle or hot enough to be soft. Try to pick a mild, cloudy day.

Extension handles are long, awkward, and floppy. Know where the hydro lines are before you start, and don't let the handle sway that way.

No matter which end of the chimney you inspect, there are three things to look for: obstructions, damage, and flammables.

Obstructions are more likely to surprise cottagers in the spring, with a room full of smoke for those who didn't inspect the chimney as part of the opening ritual. The usual culprits are critters: nesting squirrels, misguided birds, even raccoons.

Damage—broken flue tiles, fallen masonry, split seams in metal chimneys—can be spotted with a visual inspection and should be seen to ASAP. Chimney damage can put smoke in the cottage and fire where it shouldn't be.

The usual sight inside the chimney is soot and creosote. Soot is loose and dusty and comes in various shades of grey, depending on what you've been burning and at what temperature. Most of the soot will have fallen to the bottom. Creosote looks like runny black tar when it first condenses inside the flue, especially near the top where the

On a bright day, you can reflect sunlight down the flue for visual inspection.

Select a brush to fit the opening; plastic bristles for insulated chimneys and metal bristles for these clay flu tiles.

Metal stove pipes can be dismantled and cleaned outside.

chimney is coolest. Heat puffs it out into a crisp black waffle that coats the inside of the flue. It's flammable at any stage and should be scrubbed out before it becomes ⅛" thick.

Choose a brush suitable for the chimney. Metal, insulated chimneys usually have a stainless-steel liner. Use a plastic brush in these to avoid scratching the liner. Masonry chimneys, often lined with clay flue tiles, need a steel-bristle brush. Measure the inside of the flue and match the brush size to the flue, or choose one slightly bigger. A brush that is, say, ¼" too wide will work just fine. A brush that's ¼" too small can leave ¼" of creosote in the flue.

In addition to the brush, you'll need a long handle or enough screw-together extension rods to scrub the flue from top to bottom. You can skip the rods and save a few dollars by using ropes to pull the brush up and down, but that requires a helper on the other end. By the end of the chore, however, the helper at the bottom will have a very dirty face and a nasty attitude about ever helping again. Get the rods.

Seal the flue at the bottom as best you can: Close the dampers, close the fireplace, cover the woodstove with a drop cloth or an old sheet. Put on your dust mask. Then, push the brush through the flue several times, let the dust settle, and visually inspect the flue again for any stubborn patches of creosote and structural damage that might have been hidden by the creosote.

The brush should knock all the soot and most of the guck to the bottom. Shovel it away through the clean-out hole.

Ordinary metal stovepipes can be pulled apart and carried outside for cleaning. Brush them out thoroughly and check them for rust. Surface rust can be brushed off and covered with special high-temperature paint. If it goes deeper, replace the pipe.

Putting everything back together again ends on the roof, replacing the rain cap. If you haven't got one, maybe it's time. A rain cap keeps out more than rain. With a wide mesh "spark arrestor," it's equally good at keeping out raccoons, birds, and other spring obstructions.

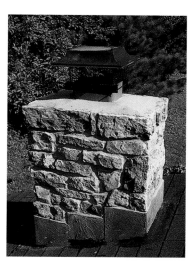

Cleaning the chimney is a dirty job, but there are compensations. You reduce the risk of a dangerous chimney fire and improve the draft in the flue (which might help that smoky fireplace). And one final thought: Tradition has it that a bride who kisses a chimney sweep on her wedding day is guaranteed good luck.

A rain cap with spark arrestor does double duty for cottagers — keeping the critters out after close-up.

FLAGPOLE

Cottagers love to show their colors. Perhaps it's the attachment to the land or the joy of staking claim to some small domain. Whatever the cause, the effect is a summer flutter of loyalties along the shore.

Tradition seems to call for a tall, slim cedar pole. Which, like many traditions, proves simpler in theory than it is in practice. For starters, it appears that very few trees really want to grow up to be flagpoles. Most tend to twist and bend; they taper from too-fat bottoms to spindly tops; they sprout limbs and spurs where we want them to be smooth. Even a perfect tree would have to be debarked and sanded to remove the snags and splinters that would shred a wind-whipped flag. And it may need regular painting to keep it from sprouting an annual crop of fresh snags and splinters.

Then, if you're lucky enough to find the perfect tree, do you really want to cut it down? Especially if it has to be delimbed, debarked, detapered, and painted to the point that nobody can tell that it was a tree? At best, the perfectly shaped, tall, slim, cedar flagpole will look exactly like one of those metal poles that comes in a box with all the hardware.

We left the forest alone and found this 18' pole in the Yellow Pages, under "Flagpoles." It comes dismantled in three sections, with hardware and an 18" ground socket. The material choices (apart from the perfect tree) include aluminum, steel, and fiberglass. You'll also have a choice of heights and a choice of mountings.

The material of choice is between you and your budget, but keep in mind that steel is prone to rust if it's not kept painted; aluminum is more vulnerable to dents and bends.

Height is first a question of aesthetics. What fits into the landscape? Secondly, match the height of the pole to the size of the flag. An oversized flag can damage, or even bend, a too-small pole, especially in wet or windy weather. Most manufacturers indicate maximum flag sizes for their poles.

The choice of mounting determines how

Swivel Base

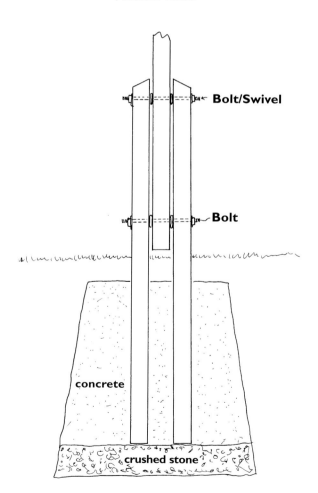

much work will be involved in the installation and maintenance. The most complicated is a swivel base: two short posts set in concrete, with the flagpole mounted between them on a rod or a long, heavy bolt, with a second bolt to hold it in the upright position. You can swivel the whole pole down to ground level to unsnarl ropes, paint, or whatever. Maintenance is a breeze, but installation is tricky. If your heart is set on a wooden pole, the swivel base is the only real option. Oh, I suppose you could fix a wooden pole solidly into the ground, but that means you'd have to shinny up the thing to unsnarl ropes or paint—and shinnying loses its appeal about the time puberty sets in.

A hollow pole can be mounted with a sleeve or socket base. The stubby sleeve, like the socket, is set in concrete. The sleeve mounting sticks up above ground while the socket ends flush with the lawn. The hollow pole slides over the sleeve or into the socket. You can take the pole down for maintenance by lifting it off the sleeve, or out of the socket, but removal does mean lifting the pole and manhandling it up and down. The hollow poles aren't particularly heavy, but you do have to watch out for power lines and picture windows anytime you're waving a 20' metal pole in the air.

We chose a socket base here,

but installation of a sleeve base proceeds exactly the same way. Begin by digging a hole, which is half the answer to the question of where to put the flagpole. Of course you want the pole away from the flag-eating trees, visible from the cottage, and far enough from habitat to take the worry out of lightning strikes. But "digging" can be problematic in cottage country. So, consider all of the usual siting criteria, and then look for a pocket of soil.

For an 18" socket, we dug a hole 2' deep and about 2' in diameter at the top (set the top layer of sod aside for later replacement).

TWO FIXED-BASE OPTIONS

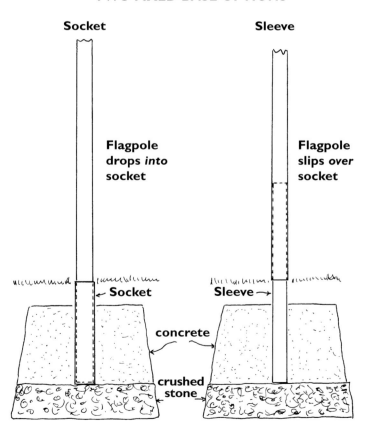

**A base of crushed rock in the bottom
of the hole helps the drainage.**

Widen the hole toward the bottom for extra stability. Fill the bottom 6" of the hole with crushed rock—for drainage—then tamp it hard and level.

Now comes the finicky part. The socket has to be set perfectly vertical before the concrete goes in the hole around it. Even a tiny misalignment at the base will be a noticeable lean at the top of a 20' pole. Unless you're flying the Pisan flag, take time to set the socket straight. Here's how:

1. Drive three stakes in the ground about 6' away from the excavation and spaced an equal distance apart.

2. Tie a string to each stake.

3. Set the socket on the crushed rock base, centered in the excavation.

4. Insert the first section of the flagpole in the socket.

5. Tie the three strings from the stakes to the top of the pole section (if the pole is too slippery to hold the string, jam a piece of wood in the top and tie the strings to that).

6. Adjust the strings to pull the pole section perfectly vertical.

7. Check it with a plumb bob or level.

Now you can mix the concrete. We used bagged premix for convenience's sake. The directions (add water and stir) are on the bag.

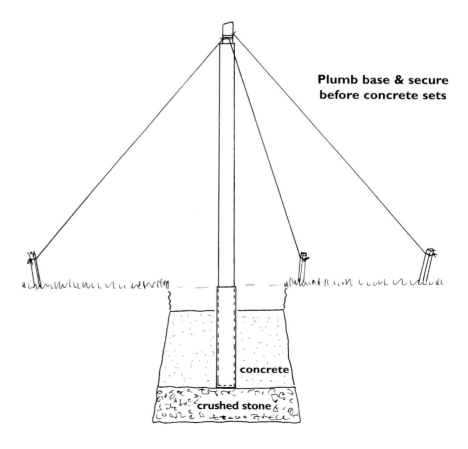

**Plumb base & secure
before concrete sets**

concrete

crushed stone

This hole took about five bags.

Carefully prod the concrete into the hole. And try not to nudge the socket aside in the process. Fill the hole about ⅔ full, leaving 4-6" at the top so that, later, you can replace the sod.

Now, while the concrete is still soft, recheck the vertical alignment of the pole. This is your last chance to correct mistakes! Got it right? Good! Tie up the dog, divert tag-playing children, and warn any wandering adults that you've planted poison ivy all around the hole. Do whatever it takes to keep trippers and stumblers away from the delicately upright pole until the next day, when the concrete will be hard enough to take over the task from the strings.

It will take at least three days for the concrete to cure. But by the morning after the pour it will be at least solid enough to remove the strings and stakes and restore the old sod. Just don't stomp the sod back into place with too much vigor since you could still dislodge the socket with such high-impact landscaping. Wash the soil back into place with a gentle hosing instead. The water will actually help the concrete cure.

Retrieve the first section of pole from its socket and assemble the flagpole on the ground. Standard fittings include a cleat to tie the rope at people height, a pulley which bolts to the pole near the top, and—sometimes—a finial to decorate the tip. When the

Plumb the first section of pole and tie it upright with strings before pouring concrete around the sleeve.

ground assembly is complete, slip the rope through the pulley, pull the loose ends even, and secure them to the cleat.

Now raise the pole upright and drop it into the socket (or slide it over the sleeve). Sounds easy, but check overhead for power lines and limbs first. If you have any doubts, get some help.

Attaching the flag requires two toggles or clips. You can buy inexpensive plastic clips from any flag dealer or whittle your own wooden toggles. Just make the toggles small enough to slip through the grommets at the back of the flag.

Slide the clips onto the free ends of the rope, push them 18-24" along, and tie each one in place with a loose knot. Then tie the free ends of the rope securely together. Adjust the two clips until they are one width of the flag apart (i.e., for a 3 x 5' flag the clips should be 3' apart), then tighten the knots that

Leave room above the concrete to restore the sod.

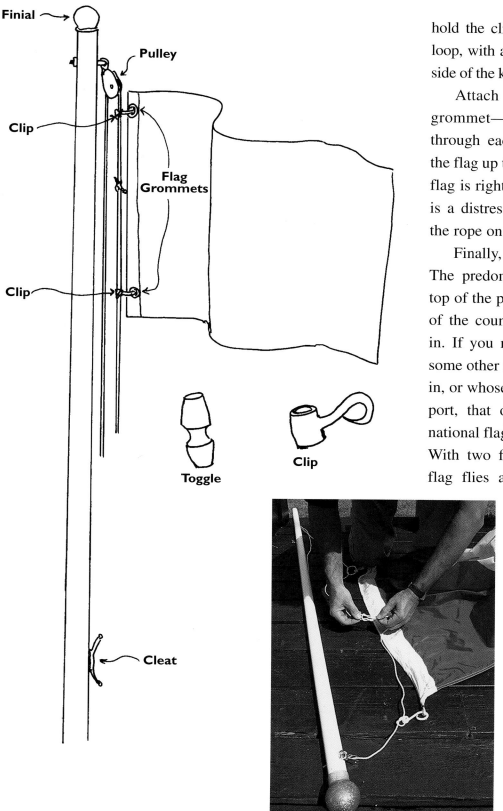

Finial

Pulley

Clip

Flag Grommets

Clip

Toggle

Clip

Cleat

hold the clips. The rope is now a loop, with a clip fastened on either side of the knot that closes the loop.

Attach a clip to each flag grommet—or slip a toggle through each grommet—and run the flag up the pole. Make sure the flag is right-side up (upside down is a distress signal). Then tie off the rope on the cleat.

Finally, a word on protocol. The predominant position at the top of the pole belongs to the flag of the country you happen to be in. If you must fly the colors of some other country you were born in, or whose soccer team you support, that one goes beneath the national flag or on a separate pole. With two flagpoles, the national flag flies at the observer's left. With three flagpoles, the national flag flies on the center pole.

Ignoring the etiquette won't get you hauled off to jail, but it will certainly irritate your neighbors.

With the clips on loosely, tie the two free ends of the halyard.

STILTS

Rip one pair of stilts from a single 2 x 4

foot rest

foot rest

Kids get bored. Even at the cottage. They get tired of the little kid toys before they're old enough to drive the big kid toys. When boredom hits your younger set, consider this simple project for some homemade fun that doesn't require a shopping mall and half of grade six. All you need are four screws and a 2 x 4. Unless, of course, you want to make another pair for yourself. Why should the kids have all the fun? Anyway, an extra pair will resolve the arguments over whose turn it is.

Begin by cutting two footrests (two fee-trests?) from one end of the 2 x 4. Lop off a chunk 6-8" long, at an angle somewhere between 30° and 45°. The cut-off piece is one footrest. Place it back on the cut end of the board, flip it so the angles match, and mark across the square end. If you cut on the mark, you'll have two matching footrests, even if you didn't measure a thing.

If you have to rip the legs with a circular saw, place wedges in the cut to avoid pinching the saw.

The rest of the 2 x 4 is for the legs. And unless you're extremely adept, you'll need two. In other words, rip the 2 x 4 in half. The safest way is on a table saw. If you don't have a table saw at the cottage, rip the board with a circular saw. Mark a line down the middle, clamp the board in the vise, and follow the line. Remember to put wedges into the cut as you go so the vise doesn't squeeze the two sides of the cut closed and jam the saw, or lose its grip on the board. If all else fails, buy two 2 x 2s.

If these stilts are for beginners, attach the footrest low—no more than 12" off the ground

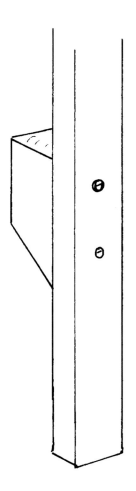

to start. Once they get the hang of it, raise it as high as you dare. Or as high as they dare.

Use two 3 ½" screws for each footrest, and predrill to avoid splitting the short blocks. Even in predrilled holes, these long screws can be hard to turn. The secret is to wipe each screw across a bar of wet soap to lubricate it on the way in. And countersink the screws to avoid scraped ankles.

You can trim the tops of the legs for height. But keep in mind the possibility of raising the footrests later. With the footrest in its highest position, there should be enough stilt above it to reach from the user's foot to the top of the shoulder. "Measuring" is a simple matter of turning the stilt upside down to ensure that the upside down footrest is at least shoulder high.

Sand everything carefully, especially along the middle of the stilt where the user has to grip. It is the hands—not the feet—that do the walking here.

There are only two tricks to walking on stilts, and the first is to forget everything you learned since your toddler days about lifting your foot to take a step. Push down (lightly) with your foot, and use your hand to lift the stilt, against the foot's pressure. If the foot tries to take a normal step, you'll step right off the stilt. Remember that when it comes time to dismount.

The other trick is to trust your instinctive balance. These things don't have size 12 bottoms and toes for balance, so you have to keep moving. For practice, rock back on your

Pre-drill the screw holes to avoid splitting the little foot rest with the big screws.

heels (toes off the ground) and try to stand still without the help of your toes. Your instinctive balance will soon have you moving from heel to heel, making little adjustments even to stand in one spot. That's exactly what you do on stilts.

Getting up takes a little trial and error. Tuck a stilt under each arm. They should pass under the armpit and end up behind the shoulder. Bend your elbows a bit, and pull them in close to the body so the stilts can't get away at the top. And grasp the stilts with your thumbs in front and your fingers behind. The footrests are in front of you, turned in to face one another. Start with one foot up on a footrest, then push off with the other foot and plant it immediately on the other footrest. And don't stop to celebrate—start rocking back and forth for balance.

The usual mistake is to forget to plant your second foot on the footrest. The second mistake is to push off too hard and step right through the stilts, or push off too softly and not have the momentum to get up.

If getting started proves a problem, try starting from a step or a low bench, something the same height as the footrest. This adds a bench to the danger of toppling backward, but it seems to help beginners gain confidence.

Once up, just keep rocking back and forth, and remember to use your hands. You'll soon be setting up obstacle courses, racing, and jousting. It may be the most fun you'll ever have with a 2 x 4. Oh, and don't forget to let the kids have a turn, too.

SCREENED PORCH

Lakeside builders knew where to put the verandah: under a shady roof, on the edge of a cooling breeze, close to refreshments, and front row center to the best view of the lake. For people, it's a great place to sit. For mosquitos, it's a great place to snack. Indeed, the only way to improve on a great verandah is to screen out those pesky mosquitos...without sacrificing the breeze or the view.

Every verandah is different, so framing dimensions and quantities of material won't mean much from one place to the next. But there is a common starting point—the choice of screening material. First, buy the strongest mesh within your budget. Lighter screening is cheaper but more prone to tear or sag.

Then there's the question of width. A standard roll of screening is 4' wide. However, the span from the floor of the verandah up to the beam that supports the roof is probably closer to 7', and some cottagers will be reluctant to give up 3' of that view. Here are the trade-offs:

1. You can run the screening vertically rather than horizontally and keep the floor-to-ceiling view. However, screening has to be supported along its edges, and the vertical solution will break up the vista with a "post" every 4'.

2. You can break the bank and order extra-wide screening, but you're unlikely to find a 7' width at any price; and even if you could, you'd spend even more time worrying about sags, snags, and tears across that greatly unsupported screen.

3. You can add a horizontal support along the bottom edge of a 4' screen and then fill in below that with another swathe of screen or a more solid skirting.

We compromised, spending a little more on a wider 5' roll of screen, and filling in at the bottom with a skirting of tongue-and-groove pine. The solid skirting does block part of the view, but only a view of the grass. Try it. Tie a string from one verandah post to another, 4' or 5' from the top. Now sit in your favorite chair and see how much scenery you'll be missing below the string. Not much? Go for the solid skirting.

You can protect the kick space from feet and rockers, without sacrificing any of the view

There's a good reason why builders call this bottom part of the wall "kick space." That's where the tricycles, dogs, cats, brooms, furniture, and—yes—toes do all their damage. Fly screen is designed to stop a hovering bug. It doesn't stand a chance against a toddler in overdrive. A 1" pine board is better equipped than a fine mesh screen to survive the wear and tear.

FRAMING

If the existing porch has a roof, a floor, some posts, and a wall or two, the important structural framing has already been done. We merely have to add enough light framing to hold the screen, the skirting, and a door. Here, the two existing posts were square 6 x 6s. By attaching the screen to the outer faces of the posts, in a long, one-piece, horizontal wrap, we can use the posts as the main elements of the framing.

We do have to add horizontal framing between the posts, along the top and bottom edges of the screened space, using pressure treated 2 x 6s. The 2 x 6" lumber matches the width of the existing posts, and the extra heft helps to keep the frame rigid over the long (16') span between the posts. Over a shorter span, we might have used 2 x 4s.

There are two keys things to remember while positioning the framing. First, align the outer edges of the framing lumber flush with the outer faces of the posts. This will allow us to staple the mesh to posts and frame in one smooth wrap. Second, be meticulous about keeping top and bottom supports arrow straight and spaced a constant distance apart.

FRAMING GUIDE

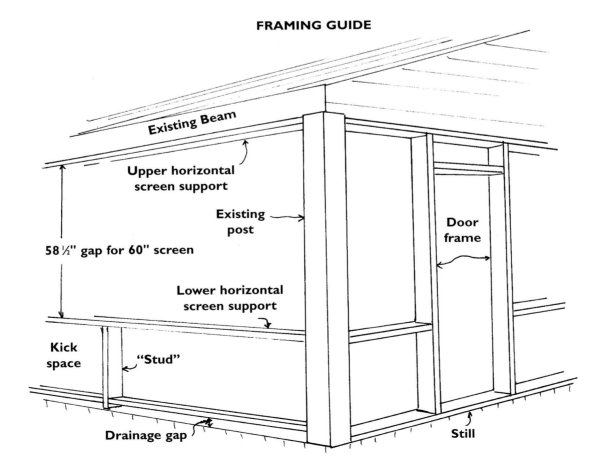

The added framing doesn't have to carry much weight, but must provide solid support for the screen, along its top and bottom edges.

Here, the old roof beam sagged and wavered up and down with age. The screen isn't flexible in that direction; the edge of the screen has to follow a straight line. So, when we added the upper support for the screen, we used a taut string as our guide and shimmed the 2 x 6 to follow the string, not the beam. Likewise, we added a couple of short vertical "studs" under the lower screen support, to take out the bounce and keep it string straight.

Space the two horizontal screen supports a constant distance apart, i.e., the width of the screen, minus 1 ½". Here, for our 60" screen, the lower support is set exactly 58 ½" from the top support. A 58 ½" opening will leave a ¾" overlap, top and bottom, to staple the screen to the 2 x 6s.

Framing at floor level depends on what the floor is made of. On a wooden deck, with gaps between the floor boards, you could nail a bottom sill directly to the deck, keeping the outer edge of the sill flush with the outer edge of the posts. On a solid floor, you'll have to allow for drainage under the bottom sill by raising it slightly. If the sill rests on concrete, separate the two materials with a

strip of "sill gasket" to help keep the wood dry even when the concrete is not.

Framing for the door starts with the door itself. A screen door is a common off-the-shelf item at any building supply store, but they do come in several widths. First select the door, then plan the opening ¼" wider than the door. Install the sill and the topmost framing member (omitting, for now, the piece that will hold the bottom edge of the screen). Fasten the uprights either side of the door opening, nailed solidly to the sill at floor level, and to the topmost framing member. Again, keep the door frame flush with the horizontal framing so you can staple the mesh right to the door frame. Fill in at either side of the door frame with the horizontal supports for the lower edge of the mesh. Add the horizontal piece across the top of the door opening and make the opening ¼" taller than the door.

SCREENING

Snap chalk lines along the centers of the top and bottom supports. The distance between the two chalk lines should be exactly the width of the screen. If we fasten the top edge of the screen along the upper chalk line, the bottom edge of screen should end up at the center of its support, with solid wood behind to hold the staple.

Stapling the screen is a job for four hands—two to hold the roll of screen, one to operate the stapler, and one to pull the edge of screening tautly into position. The least inattention will leave a wrinkle that will haunt you for the rest of the summer.

Start in an upper corner and tack 5-6' along the top. Then pull the bottom taut to its line, check to be sure that the grid of mesh is perfectly square—not pulled aside in a diagonal distortion—then tack the same 5-6' along the bottom. Use ¼" staples and don't overdo it. If you arrive at the corner post with a wrinkle, you might want to extract a few staples to straighten the mesh. When it's tight (not baggy) and straight (not wrinkled), you can go back and fill in staples every 6".

Wrap the mesh right around the porch. Don't worry about covering the door. You can cut out the door opening later, when the mesh is secure on all its supports. Fiberglass screen, and the lighter aluminum meshes, can be trimmed with a utility knife.

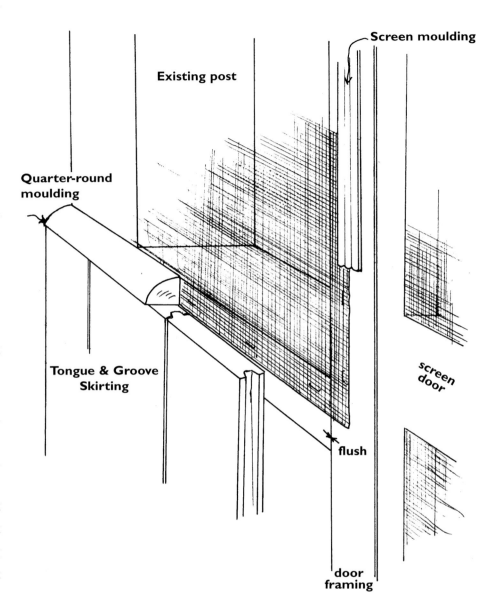

SKIRTING

Fill in the kick space with whatever matches the rest of the cottage. Chipboard and pressboard are inexpensive fillers, but they don't stand up well to the weather. Here, we used 1" pine, fastened top and bottom with finishing nails.

Avoid any temptation to fasten the skirting boards over the edge of the screen. Yes, an overlap would give more nailing room, but consider the future difficulties. The screen will almost certainly be damaged before the skirting wears out. If the mesh isn't nailed under the skirting, it will be a simpler task to pull off a damaged screen and replace it.

The exposed edges of screen can be covered with standard moldings. A ¾ inch "quarter-round" piece will cap the top edge of the skirting and cover the bottom edge of screen. Flat "screen" molding will cover stapled edges around the doorway and where mesh meets the cottage. The moldings improve the appearance and help hold the screen in place. If you use light finishing nails, the moldings can be removed should you have to replace the screen.

Add "quarter round" molding to the top of the kick-space panels. This covers the bottom edge of the screen.

FINISHING TOUCHES

The door needs a couple of hinges and a latch, plus a spring attachment if your guests are careless about closing doors behind them.

Light screen door hinges can be mounted on the surface of the door frame—no need to chisel hinge recesses. Mount the hinges first, swing the door into the closed position, then add 1 x 2 strips on the sill behind the door, up the jambs, and at the top. Place them against the door, but nail them into the frame. These simple "stops" close the last gap and keep the door from swinging through the opening. The latch and spring go on last.

Now consider other routes the mosquitos might choose. Check the roof line for gaps between the rafters. Can the bugs reach the porch through the crawl space under the cottage? Through the cracks in a wooden deck? Staple screening across any roof line gaps and to the underside of the deck. Those who are squeamish about crawling under a cottage porch may be tempted to spend a little more money and lay plywood or carpet atop the open decking. Bad choice. A solid floor subverts the drainage, and standing water may spoil the floor.

There's some dispute over the best time to paint. The shortcut artists insist that it makes more sense to paint the framing before the screen goes on, in order to reach those parts of the framing that will be covered by the screen but visible through it. On the other hand, those resigned to the inevitable leave the painting until last, on the assumption that the whole thing will have to be repainted eventually and the under-screen parts will be inaccessible then anyway. Suit yourself.

HANGING
A
HAMMOCK

The perfect spot has a view, a breeze and a bit of shade.

A swaying hammock takes center stage in many an imagined idyll—sultry under a pair of languorous palms or slinky through a needled veil of aromatic pine. Whenever dreams include a water view, a breeze, a book, or a lover, chances are that there is a hammock in the picture.

The fantasy founders on reality's shoal when it comes to the trees on which this dream is supposed to swing. The perfect pair of hammock trees are a rare breed indeed. Ideally, they should offer shade and yet be open to a breeze, provide privacy while permitting a view, be close enough to hear the waves but far enough to avoid the splash, be a hammock's length apart and sturdy enough to withstand your weight.

Then, having found the perfect pair of trees, the would-be idyller must consider the prospect of injuring these ideal specimens with whatever hooks, nails, or horrible things it might take to hang the hammock up—and to hang it up tightly enough to take the "fall" out of falling asleep.

I once thought that the kindest way to hang a hammock would be with a rope (assuming I could learn to tie something tighter than a slip knot). But the tree people tell me that the rope might not, after all, be gentler than the screw. Justin Starkweather, who makes hammocks at Sitting Pretty, near Hopetown, Ontario, says that tying a rope around a tree can cut the circulation of the sap and eventually lead to its death. The tree's "arteries," if you like, those sapwood cells

The trick is to find two trees the right distance apart.

which pass water and nutrients from the roots to the top, lie just under the bark. A tight girdle of anything can lead to the botanical equivalent of a rope burn or a choke hold.

A slip collar at least reduces the stranglehold to fewer pressure points. Screw eyelets into scraps of wood, pass a rope through the eyelets, space the scraps (or pads) evenly around the trunk, and tie the rope behind the tree. The pads hold the rope away from the bark. With no weight on it, the collar slips easily up and down the trunk for height adjustments and is loose enough to leave some growing room. Add the weight of the hammock and idler, however, and the collar tightens its grip.

It's better than the noose, but the collar still rubs the bark at every point where the pads touch. And the possibility of unplanned slippage can give the napper a nervous tic.

If all those complications threaten to worry the fun out of an afternoon idyll, take some comfort from the assurance of the tree guys that there is little harm done by putting one hook into a tree...as long as you do it right.

First pick a big enough tree. Some hammock makers suggest that a 6" diameter tree is an acceptable minimum. There are other factors, however. If you're a heavyweight, or if you're hanging a wide, two-people hammock, or if you're hoping for something more vigorous than a nap, look for a bigger tree. Some species are weaker and more shallow-rooted than others. A 6" oak might suffice; a 6" poplar would not. When in doubt, try shaking the tree. If you can move the trunk with just two hands, your whole weight yanking on the hammock hook might be too much for the poor thing.

Now determine a proper height for the hooks. This depends, in part, on the hammock and, in part, on the spacing of the trees. The big, double-wide hammock you see here measures 13' from ring to ring. Our two trees are almost 13' apart. So, when we first hang it up, the hammock will be almost horizontal. However, as soon as I get in, it will sag. Over time, the ropes will stretch and the hammock

will sag even more. If we don't hang it high enough in the beginning, we'll end up bumping our saggy bottoms on the ground. Setting these hooks about 5 ½' high will leave just enough swinging room underneath. If the trees were closer together, the hammock would slack lower in the middle, and we would have to raise the hooks to compensate. Likewise, if the trees were farther apart, we would have to add short links of chain to span the gaps from the rings to the trees; that longer suspension would sag lower in the middle, and we would again have to raise the hooks to compensate. Trial and error, with temporary rope ties, will help you determine the right hook height for your trees and your hammock.

When you have decided how high the support has to be, drill a guide hole for the screw hook (a screw hook usually comes with the hammock). Select a drill bit smaller in diameter than the diameter of the screw. A ⅜" screw hook, for example, will hold nicely in a ¼" guide hole. Drill upward at a slight angle so that weight in the hammock will try

You can make a simple slip collar from scraps of wood. (above)

It's loose enough to adjust and leave some growing room, but tightens when you put any weight on the hook. (right)

A single screw hook does little damage to the tree

to pull the screw straight out of its socket and not yank it down against the bottom edge of the hole (which might split the wood below).

Turn the screw into the guide hole until all that shows is the hook. A little wet soap along the threads will ease the turning. And if the turning is still too tough for fingers, insert a rod or a long screwdriver through the hook to provide the extra torque required.

The hook is a kinder, gentler support for the simple reason that it's only one point on the tree's circumference. It interrupts only one small part of the feeding mechanism instead of choking it off. It's akin, they say, to tapping a maple in spring. The maple eventually seals off the hole and grows over it. Similarly, the hammock tree will grow tighter around the screw and will eventually grow right over it, or

Angle the hole so the weight of the hammock will try to pull the hook straight out, instead of levering it down against the edge of the hole.

"swallow" it. In fact, always use extra care when cutting a tree in a spot so perfect that it might have once held a hammock. There could be hidden hooks in the wood that might damage a saw chain or, worse, break it.

The more immediate danger might appear to be the process of getting in safely. Stretched taut and flat, the newly hung hammock looks more of a challenge than it really is. Forget the ladder. Just back into the center of the thing. Reach behind you and pull the outer edge down and under your hips. Roll back and swing your feet around.

Hammock manufacturers offer a wide choice of sizes, colors, and styles. Woven rope hammocks are cooler than the old-fashioned solid canvas ones. Natural fibers may be more prone to mildew and rot. Synthetic fibers are waterproof but may stretch at different rates. Dacron is stronger than olefin but costs more. Ask about ultraviolet resistance and maintenance if any. Some manufacturers offer freestanding hammock supports, in case you don't have the perfect pair of hammock trees, or in case they aren't growing in the right spot.

Whatever you choose, one thing is certain: You'll find a comfy snoozing position every time. In fact, if there was a saint dedicated to the cottage nap, the hammock would be her shrine. Which is why I've named this one my idyll idle idol.

CANOE
RACK

MATERIALS

2 x 4 cedar
8' long
9 pieces

#8 screws
4" long
16

#8 screws
3" long
8

¼" carriage bolts
3 ½" long
18

nuts
18

washers
18

½" dowels

It isn't just the canoe. It's all those water toys—the kayak, wind surfer, dingy, sails, and paddles—too light to leave in the water and too awkward to put away each night. They end up as a clutter by the shore. Worse, they suffer from being left on the ground.

The challenge is to make a storage rack strong enough to hold all these water thingies off the ground, and at the same time keep the rack light enough to move around. That way, we can leave the rack down by the water's edge all summer and carry it inside, or out of sight, when we close the cottage in the fall.

"Lightweight strength" doesn't have to be a contradiction in terms. The light

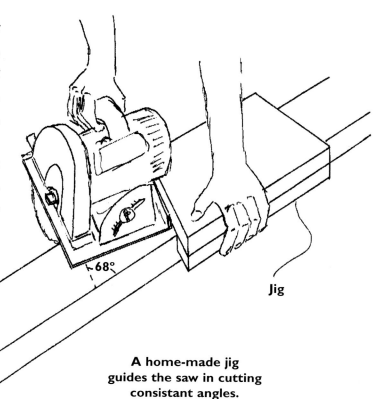

Jig

A home-made jig guides the saw in cutting consistant angles.

END ASSEMBLY:

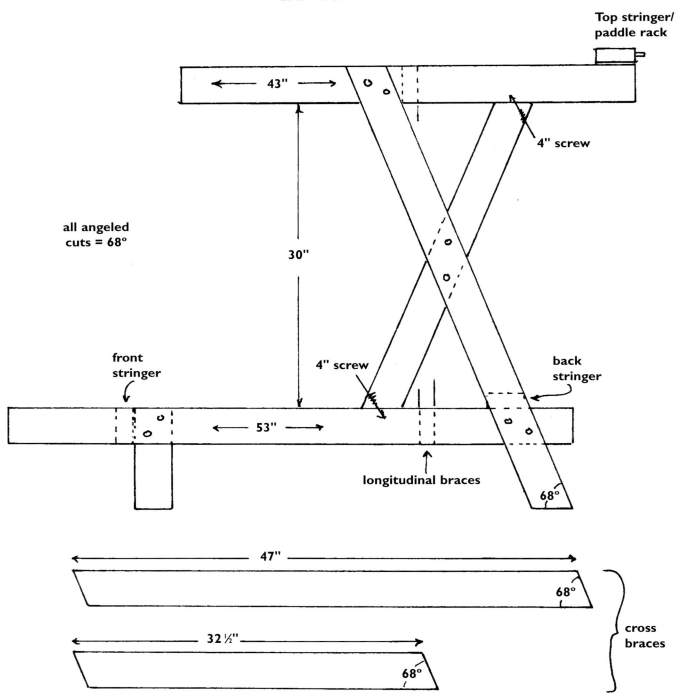

Top stringer/paddle rack

43"

4" screw

all angeled cuts = 68°

30"

front stringer

4" screw

back stringer

53"

longitudinal braces

68°

47"

68°

32 ½"

68°

cross braces

part starts with 2 x 4 cedar, and no foundation or heavy underpinnings. The strength comes from cross-bracing rather than from heavy timbers.

There's no magic in the length of the arms that hold the watercraft. We designed these supporting arms to be 43" and 53" long (top and bottom) just so we could cut both arms from one 8' board. Make either set of arms longer if you have a wide-beam boat, or trim them shorter if the ends stick out unnecessarily.

Begin by cutting out all the pieces according to the plans, except for the front legs and the top stringer (the paddle rack). We'll make front legs from the cut-off scrap. For now, leave the top stringer as a full-length 8' board

For simplicity's sake, all the angled cuts are designed to be 68°. One cutting jig serves all. To make the jig, cut the end of a scrap board at 68° on a table saw, or lay out the angle with a protractor and cut it by hand. Screw a piece of 1 x 2 to the long side of the angled board, and you've made a jig. Place the jig on the board to be cut, pull it tight against the far side of the board with one hand, and saw with the other hand, using the angled jig as a guide.

Build one end assembly with two cross braces and the two horizontal arms. And don't worry about the missing front leg. We'll get to that later. Tighten the bolts until the washers compress the wood. And offset the bolts diagonally across the grain as shown, for strength.

Use the first end assembly as a template to build the second. If you like, you can even

clamp the loose pieces to the finished assembly while you mark them and drill them for fastening. This will ensure that the two ends match.

Stand the two end assemblies erect, and join them by attaching the bottom stringers, front and back. Note that the back stringer rests atop the bottom arms and so is cut 3" longer than the front stringer, which fits between the bottom arms. Use longer 3 ½" or 4" screws for the front stringer as these will have to hold in the weaker end grain.

The end assembly is still missing one leg. That goes on last, to level the rack on uneven ground.

Don't cut the top stringer, the paddle rack, to its final length just yet. Clamp it across the top arms, or tack it with temporary nails. Fitting the longitudinal braces and squaring everything up might require some adjustments which a permanent stringer at the top would impede.

Attach one of the long angled braces at the bottom, and clamp it, tack it, or have

The long braces, crossed and bolted in the middle, will stop any longitudinal sway.

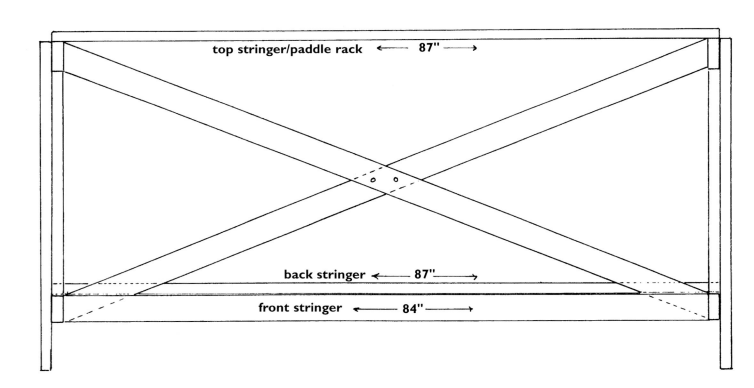

top stringer/paddle rack ← 87" →

back stringer ← 87" →

front stringer ← 84" →

long angeled braces (2)   68°

← 90½" →

somebody hold it at the other end, at the top. Attach the other angled brace at the bottom and roughly fit it at the top. The two angled braces should touch in the middle, where they cross. You can clamp them there, but don't fasten them just yet.

First check that the two end assemblies are square in all directions (this is difficult on uneven ground; use the deck, or the dock). When it all stands square, check that the top ends of the angled braces abut the top arms solidly. At this point it is still a simple matter to shift the end assemblies around to get everything square and fitted.

Satisfied? Then screw the long angled braces through the top arms. These screws also have to hold in the end grain, so use the long screws. Then bolt the long angled braces together in the middle, where they cross.

Now you can cut the top stringer to length and screw it in place. A series of paired ½" dowels along the back will hang paddles, towels, or life jackets.

Finally, find a spot to put the rack. Close to the water so the toys actually get put away is best, but "close to the water" often means uneven ground. That's why we left the front legs until last.

Stand the rack in place and prop it up more or less level. Bubble level is less important than ensuring that the supporting arms at one end are parallel to those at the other end. The rack still has some flex from end to end. If the supporting arms are flexed out of parallel, the canoe won't be evenly supported.

When it looks right, place a short piece of 2 x 4 in the front leg position and push it hard to the ground. Fasten it, check again that the two supports are parallel, and fasten the other front leg the same way.

If the position is semipermanent, go ahead and fasten the front legs to the lower arms with bolts, and screw the front stringer to the legs. But remember that if you want to move the rack into a garage or covered storage area for the winter, you might have to readjust the legs to level the supporting arms again.

**The rack is sturdy enough
to hold two craft and is still
light enough to move around.**

RETAINING WALL

MATERIALS

Stone is usually free in cottage country as long as you're willing to haul it yourself. Ask local farmers if you can pick stones from their fence rows or look for abandoned quarries. If possible pick shapes that resemble slabs more than bowling balls. And gather twice as much as you think you'll need.

Geo-blankets come in several widths and are widely available through landscape suppliers. We got this 5' width for less than a dollar per linear foot.

A retaining wall is an old idea. Stone Age do-it-yourselfers were piling up rocks to make a terrace or to hold a slope against erosion, long before the first cottage. The geo-blanket has, however, given the job a whole new twist. Indeed, if you're planning a retaining wall anywhere near the water, you might be required to use one of these fiber backings to keep the soil from washing out through the gaps between the stones.

Gaps between the stones? What about mortar, or "cement" as the stuff between the stones is sometimes—mistakenly—called? The problem is that a solid, mortared wall is a monolith—rigid, unbending. As the frost beneath it heaves unevenly, the wall has to lift as one unbending unit, or it has to break. Usually, it breaks. The only lasting solution is to build such a wall on a footing that reaches below the deepest penetration of frost, which can be 5-6' in cottage country. And if it's a retaining wall, it has to be strong enough to withstand the thrust of frost expansion in the dirt behind it. It also has to be well-drained, so it doesn't act like a dam and pile up water behind it.

If all that sounds like too much trouble for a little cottage retaining wall, it is. There is, however, a simpler solution. Build the wall dry, rock on rock, no mortar. Trust gravity to keep it up. Gravity pulls each rock

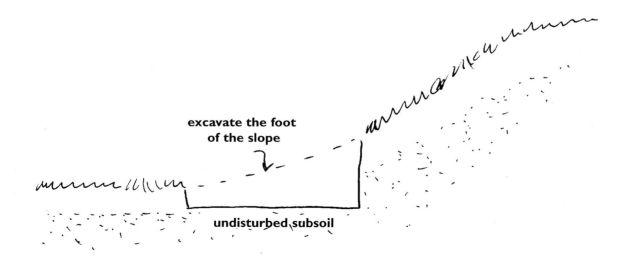

excavate the foot
of the slope

undisturbed subsoil

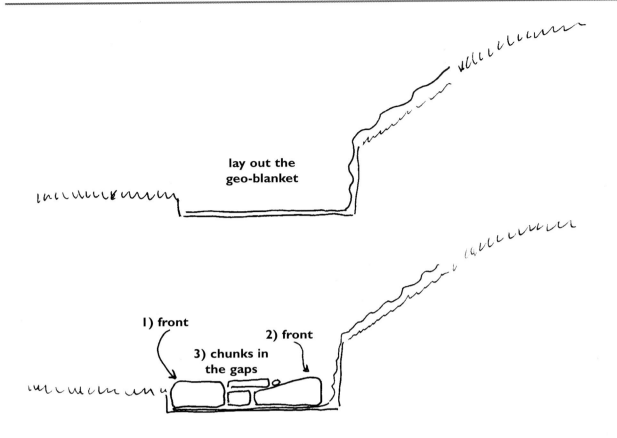

straight down onto the rocks beneath it, tightening the bond. The heavier the rock, the tighter the bond. Gravity can't pull a stone out of a well-built wall unless gravity learns to pull sideways.

When frost heaves an unmortared wall, the wall bends. The stones lift a little and then settle back more or less where they were before, with no mortar cracks to show the movement. If we lay out the wall with a wide base and a face that leans back against the hill, it will withstand the push of the dirt behind it. And the gaps between the stones let the water pass through.

The best part is that we don't have to dig a 6' hole to build a 2' wall. Usually, a wide trench, about 6" deep, is enough to remove most of the roots and loose surface soils which would compress and unbalance the wall. We want to start building on a level surface of compact, undisturbed subsoil. Dig back into the foot of the slope and pile the extra dirt to use as final backfill at the top of the wall.

The trench, or base of the wall, should be at least as wide as the wall is high. Here, we started with a base 2' wide to build a wall 2' high.

Roll out the geo-blanket along the bottom

of the trench, so that the first row of face stones will just cover the front edge of the blanket. And lay the rest over the slope, leaving some slack so the blanket can follow any lumpy bulges up the back of the wall.

Lay out the first row of stones along the face. Lay them flat—not standing on edge. Turn the straightest edge to the front. And try to keep them all the same height. If you don't have enough stones of the same height to complete the whole row, at least group common heights together to leave as few up-and-down steps as possible.

Lay out a similar row along the back of the wall. Then stuff any gaps between the front and the back with smaller rocks. That's one "course" complete.

the wall its strength. When two adjacent stones are a common height, spanning them is simple. When they're "stepped" at different heights, we have to find a mirror-image "step" stone to span them or adjust with thin filler rocks to level the base for the second course. Span, or stagger, every joint in the face below.

Try, too, to overlap from front to back. The front face and the back should not stand independent of one another. Instead, they should be tied together with an occasional rock which spans the full width or with stones that overlap from course to course.

Apart from the added complication of staggered joints, the second course proceeds in the same order as the first: front face, back,

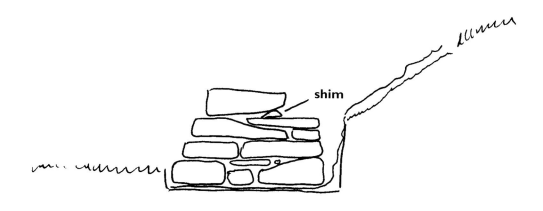

The second course makes it clear why we tried to leave the previous course with an even top. Now each stone has to rest on at least two below, spanning the joints in the lower course. It's this overlapping that gives

fill any gaps between. And, as before, try to finish at a common height.

It's a rare rock that will fit right into place without a wobble. A wobble says the rock is resting on just two points. You can wiggle it

The wall will be in a better position to resist the push from behind if you leave a wide base and slope the face into the hill.

around or turn it to try to improve stability, but once you've got it where you want it to be, fixing a wobble is as simple as providing a third point of support. Keep a "shim" pail of random flat pieces at hand. Wobble the rock down in front, and push a shim in from behind. If possible, avoid shimming in the exposed face of the wall, where the shim will eventually fall out. If you shim the wobblers at the back, inside the wall, the shim will have no place to fall.

You can break stones with a sledge or chisel, in a rude attempt to improve the fit. But chiseling is rarely worth the effort in a rustic wall like this. You'll find the hammer more useful for tapping stones into position or tightening up the shims.

Each course gets a little narrower than the one below. The back should rise vertically, but the front face steps back a little with each course. This sloped profile, leaning back against the hill, lowers the wall's center of gravity and shifts it back closer to the rear of the wall, making it much more difficult for a pushy hill to topple the wall over on its face.

Most mortarless walls that fail, come apart from the top. They've been built upside down, with the heavy rocks at the bottom and

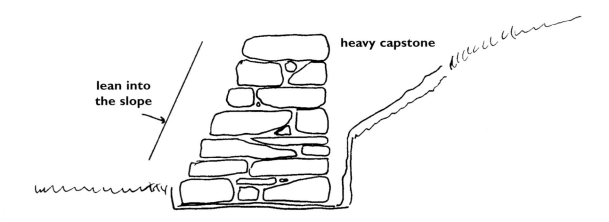

lean into the slope

heavy capstone

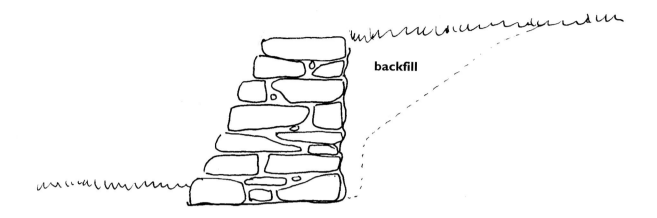

backfill

the small ones on top. Wall-walkers and lawn mowers can easily kick the smaller stones loose. Fixing the fallen would be a simple matter of picking them up and putting them back on the wall. But there's an even easier way to prevent the problem. Save the biggest stones for last, and cap the wall with these. The brutes on top will keep the little stones in place. And don't set these capstones lengthwise, along the front of the wall where they might roll off, but turn them so they cross the top of the wall.

When you've set the final course of capstones, shimmed the wobbles, and jammed the gaps with shards, pull the blanket up at the back and rake the dirt in behind it. Don't pull the blanket too tight. Instead, let the dirt push it in folds around the backs of the rocks so the rocks—not the blanket—bear the weight of the fill. Cut off the blanket at the top, or bury any excess just under the surface.

When the backfill has settled, and it may take a rain or two, plant any raw earth along the top to prevent surface erosion. And if you really want to attach the wall to the landscape, plant Virginia creeper or Boston ivy beside it.

Put the big rocks at the face and on the top, fill in behind with rubble, and use a geo-blanket to keep the dirt from washing through.

WINDOW REPAIRS

Scrape out the old putty with a chisel

There is one obscure law of the universe which limits the discovery of broken windows to long weekends, when the nearest window repair shop is sure to be 50 miles and three days away. That's three days of mosquito bites and bats, or an ugly cardboard patch duct-taped over the hole. Either way it's a pain.

Not to worry. You can replace the glass yourself. If possible, take the window out of the frame and move it down to an area where you can work without falling off a ladder. And then remove any remnants of the broken pane.

Careful, methodical do-it-yourselfers will pluck the glass shards out of the putty with pliers. The rest of us, who hadn't really planned on wasting any valuable weekend time on a nuisance chore like this, will feel better by smashing it out with a hammer. Either way, cover up: protective glasses, boots, long pants, and heavy gloves. And, if you want to save cleanup time later on, use an open garbage can as a worktable, and drop the sharp slivers straight into the can.

The tedious bit involves scraping the old putty away. On an old, weathered window, where the putty has dried out and cracked, you might be able to pry it away in chunks with a putty knife or even a screwdriver. If the putty is tougher and more tenacious than that, you can shave it away with a sharp chisel or a utility knife. Takes time, but it works. The high-tech approach requires a heat gun. It softens the old putty so you can scrape it out easily. Just remember to keep the heat off any adjacent glass by using a directional nozzle or a shield; and keep moving the heat gun to avoid scorching the wood.

With the putty out of the way, you'll see that it wasn't actually putty that held the glass in the frame, but a series of little metal clips called "glazier's points." There are two common kinds: a flat diamond shape and a flanged version. Pull out the points with small pliers—straight out, just like pulling teeth.

Sometimes, scraping gets down to the bare wood, which can suck the fresh putty dry and cause it to crack. Daub the bare bits with

**Score the glass with one
firm stroke of the cutter...**

Hold the scored glass firmly...

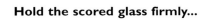

...and snap!

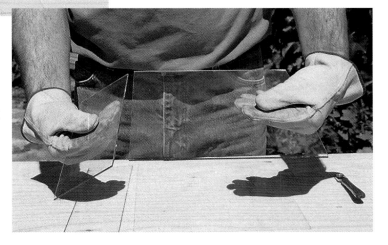

a little thinned paint, or primer, or anything to seal the raw wood. And while that's drying, we'll cut a new pane of glass to fit the hole.

CUTTING GLASS

Most of us have an odd collection of discarded glass around somewhere: old storm windows, big remnants of past broken panes, renovation castoffs. They're practically guaranteed to be the wrong size and shape, but anything bigger than the piece we need can be cut down to size. It's not the highly skilled task that it appears to be. In fact, cutting the glass to size is the simplest part of window repair.

First, measure the space to be filled. Subtract ⅛" from each dimension, to leave a little wriggling-in room. Then select a sufficiently large sheet of glass to cut. Usually, you can start with an existing corner and create the new pane with just two cuts. Don't try too hard to find a scrap that is almost the right size. Trimming a narrow edge off a piece that's just a bit too wide will be much more difficult than cutting a larger piece.

Preparation counts for more than skill. Clean the glass carefully; a smudge can cause the cutter to skip. And brush off the work surface; the tiniest bit of grit or glass chip can stress the glass and break it in the wrong place. The ideal work surface is perfectly flat and smooth, with a straight, hard edge. Use a piece of good plywood or even the kitchen table (a sheet will protect the surface).

Measure and mark the dimensions of the new pane right on the glass, using a felt-tipped pen. You will also need a straightedge and a glass cutter. The cheapest cutter (under $5) is a simple handle with notches on the side and a tiny wheel built into one end. It works fine, but not for long. Eventually, the cutter wheel dulls and skips. For under $10, you can buy one with half a dozen cutters. When one wheel dulls, you simply rotate the next one into position.

Hold the straightedge with one hand and the cutter with the other. The straightedge guides the cutter. The cutter does all the work. Hold it up straight, like a pencil, and—with about the same pressure you would use to draw a dark pencil line—score the glass all the way across. If the cutter slips, leaving an unscored gap, a drop of light oil will loosen the wheel. The only trick is to score the line all in one smooth stroke—right off the edge of the glass.

Okay, so "cutter" is a bit of a misnomer. "Scratcher" would be closer to the truth. But if the scratch is deep enough, and straight enough, it will weaken the glass along that line, and that is where it should break.

Once it's scored, position the glass so that the scratch is exactly aligned with the hard edge of the work surface underneath. Most of the glass will rest on the table, the excess will project beyond the edge. Put one (gloved) hand on the glass and grasp the projecting waste with the other hand. "Snap" off the excess with a quick, firm, downward push.

It doesn't always break exactly where you want it to. But you can improve the odds by starting with clean glass, a smooth work surface, and a free-wheeling cutter. If that isn't enough, you can use the other end of the cutter (it's often weighted for this very purpose) to tap along the underside of the scored line, weakening it even more.

Sometimes the break veers away from the line. You can chip any such bulges back to the scored line with the cutter. One of the notches on the side of the tool will fit over the edge of the glass, and a little twist will break off a small chip of glass. The result is a little rougher than a clean break, but it works.

PUTTY IN YOUR HANDS

Putty, or glazing compound, comes in cans, in caulking tubes, or in plastic bags. The difference is partly cost and partly convenience. Putty has to be pliable for application, which usually means "kneading" it in your hands to remix any separated ingredients, to warm it, and to soften it. It's a messy but not unpleasant task. The plastic bags allow you to knead the putty while it's still inside the bag, but the bags don't reseal well to keep leftovers. Canned putty can be resealed, but it still requires some hands-on mixing. Tubed putty requires a caulking gun and—because it can't be kneaded—is often runnier than canned or bagged compounds. If you're kneading by hand, you will feel the putty soften like kids' modeling clay. Roll it between your palms to make long "ropes" of putty, just the way you made clay snakes in kindergarten.

Place a thin bead of putty around the frame and then push the new glass into place with sufficient pressure to squeeze the putty out into a uniform bed. This seals the back of the glass against the wooden frame.

Fasten the bedded glass in place with glazier's points. The flanged "push points" are considerably easier to use. Lay the point flat on the glass (flanges up), with the sharp end against the wooden frame. Then place a putty knife or screwdriver against the flange and push the point into the wood, right up to the flange. Use two points on each edge or one every 12" on larger panes.

Now roll up some fatter ropes of putty and push them firmly into the angle between the glass and the frame, burying the tops of the glazier's points. Then smooth the surface by drawing the putty knife along the rough bead. Maintain enough pressure on the knife to cut a clean edge along the glass and along the top of the frame, forcing the excess putty aside. If you scrape up the ribbons of waste right away, you can knead them into a new rope for the next side.

When you've tidied up the putty surface to your satisfaction, clean the knife and your hands with mineral spirits and rehang the window. The raw putty surface will have to dry for a few days before it will be hard enough to paint. And it really should be painted to keep from weathering and cracking. That, however, is next weekend's project.

Rolling canned putty between your palms makes it soft and pliable...

Force it into the angle between the glass and the frame...

And smooth it out with a putty knife.

CONCRETE STEPS

Concrete suffers more from weather damage than from wear and tear. It's the changing seasons, the freeze/thaw cycle, and the frost pushing at it from underneath. A simple slab can ride out the heaves like a raft. But jammed up against the cottage, or bearing uneven weight, something eventually has to break.

A broken back door slab is easy enough to replace, but this time we wanted to get it right. First, we removed all the old concrete and the topsoil it had been sitting on. Loose surface soil can compress over time and allow the slab to settle unevenly. Worse, the soil acts like a sponge, holding water which later freezes and expands.

We excavated down to a layer of undisturbed subsoil, then refilled the bottom of the hole with at least 6" of clear (screened) crushed rock. The rock will allow drainage from underneath and provide a solid base for the slab. Add the rock in layers, raking, leveling, and tamping as you go. Bring the base up to within 6" of where you want the final surface of the slab to be.

The form is a simple rectangle of 2 x 6s, nailed at the corners. Wipe some oil on the inner surfaces to make the form easier to separate from the concrete later. Set it on the base of crushed rock, and square the corners. Don't be tempted to use the cottage as one side of the form; a little separation will allow the slab to move if it must, without also trying to move the attached building.

The step, like any hard surface adjacent to the cottage, should be sloped away from the wall for drainage. Set the inside edge of the form up to an inch higher than the outer edge. You can adjust the height and slope of the form by reraking the crushed rock surface.

When the form is in the right position, brace it from the outside with stakes. Add more crushed rock outside the perimeter as well. Wet concrete will try to push out the sides of the best-built form.

Concrete forms are simple, but they must be sturdy. A base of crushed rock helps the drainage.

Now comes the fun: mixing concrete. A little job like this doesn't justify a $300 mixer. It certainly doesn't justify truckloads of sand and gravel (the low-budget way to buy the ingredients). The little jobs are, however, tailor-made for bagged premix. Each bag contains sand, aggregate, and cement in standard proportions, plus instructions (add water). You can also tell your building supply dealers what volume of finished concrete you want, and they can send you away with the right number of bags.

If you've got a wheelbarrow, or even a hard, flat surface like a driveway, empty a bag or two of the concrete mix into a heap. Then use a clean hoe or a shovel to make a crater in the top of the heap. Pour some clean water into the crater. Gently pull the rim of the crater into the lake and start turning the sides into the wet middle. When the water is gone and the volcano has been reduced to an unmixable muddle of dusty blobs and damp patches, make another crater and add a little more water. Add less water each time, until the mix is uniformly damp and grey, sliding off the shovel easily. It should be the consistency of tapioca pudding: gritty, soft, slumping but holding a little bit of shape. I thought it couldn't get any simpler than that. But it did.

This new, plastic, barrel mixer has built-in mixing vanes along the sides and sells for under $50. It takes one bag of premix, and the screw-on top also measures the water. You dump in the ingredients, tighten the top, tip the barrel onto its side, and roll it around the yard.

Dump the mix into the forms and start the next batch right away. As you dump in subsequent batches, use the shovel to blend each new batch in with the rest. Chop and prod to flow the concrete like chunky lava into all the corners. You'll have to work quickly to dump the last batch before the first one becomes too stiff to meld with the rest.

No matter how you mix it, wet concrete is sensitive to weather and time. On a hot or windy day the mix stiffens faster. You'll have to add extra water to the mix, wet the crushed rock base, shade the job site, and work extra fast to keep up. On a cool, cloudy day, use less water and take your time.

When the last batch is in, go all around the inside of the forms with the shovel, chop-

Finish with a wooden float, and then add a non-slip texture by brushing the still-damp surface

ping and slicing, working out all the air pockets. Tapping the outside of the form with a hammer also helps to fill the voids.

Now level the top—don't trowel it! Not yet anyway. For now, all we want to do is scrape off the excess, or "screed" it. Use any scrap of lumber long enough to reach from one side of the form to the other. Rest it on edge, on top of the form, and "saw" back and forth, pushing a wave of concrete ahead. Push the wave of excess right over the end of the form. You may have to screed back and forth several times to fill all the dips. But don't overdo it. Too much fuss will bring puddles of water to the surface...and so will finishing it too soon.

Leave it alone until the surface is too hard to push your thumb right in but still soft enough to leave an impression. That might take an hour on a hot day, or longer if it's cool. Start with a wooden float. Sweep it from side to side in broad, overlapping arcs. Think of buttering bread. And raise the leading edge ever so slightly, just enough to keep it from digging in or dragging up stones. It feels rough at first—like ironing rocks—but soon starts to glide as the surface stones settle just a little and a thin skim of sand and cement rises to the top.

If it continues to feel rough and dry beneath the float, add a little pressure. If, on the other hand, the float puddles water to the surface right away, leave it to dry a little longer. The float should leave a damp slick on the surface, not soup.

We don't want a glassy smooth finish on a step, so there's no need for a steel trowel on this job. Even the float can leave a step dangerously smooth. When you've finished the surface with the float, leave it to dry for another half hour or so, and then add some texture with a stiff-bristled broom or whisk. Hold the broom almost upright, sweeping long overlapping strokes across the surface. Don't dig in; use just enough pressure to leave a pattern of tiny furrows behind.

If you have an edging trowel, slide it along the inside of the form—carefully at first, lest you dig out a stone, then a little more pressure, back and forth until the trowel leaves a damp slick on the newly rounded edge.

The rest is patience and understanding the most important fact about concrete: It is supposed to cure, not dry. No matter how illogical it sounds, the object now is to keep the concrete damp. Its strength comes from a chemical reaction between the water and the cement. When the water is gone, the reaction stops. The longer we can keep it damp, the harder it gets. So put a sheet of plastic over it and leave it alone for at least three days.

We can pull the forms off then, and the step will be hard enough to use. But if you hose it down and throw the plastic back over it for an extra week, it will only get stronger.

BARBEQUE

MATERIALS

grill(s)
   big enough for your standard cookout

hanger hardware
   8 angle braces or corner braces
   16 nuts
   16 flathead bolts

2" firebrick
   16

refractory cement
   1 can (also called stove/furnace cement)

mortar mix
   10 bags, approximately

concrete mix
   10 bags for barbecue base, approximately

concrete mix
   2 bags for countertops
   (or substitute precast concrete slabs)

   1 bag for firebox base
   (or substitute precast concrete slabs)

Barbecue design begins with the grill. The rest, including the stone, is only there to hold the grill above the fire.

We selected two grills to give us the option of one big cooking surface or two cooking surfaces at different heights. Each measured 14 x 10 ¾". The firebox is designed to fit around the grill space, with a little extra room to allow for hangers at the sides. The base is designed to bring the top of the firebox—and thus the grill—to 36", the standard height for a kitchen stove. Add the width of countertops, either side of the firebox, to establish the overall width of the structure.

We formed these 30 x 12" countertops by

FRONT VIEW

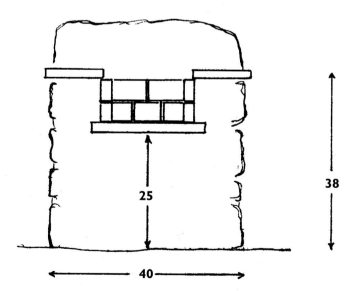

setting 1 x 2s on edge and nailing scrap plywood underneath. Make sure the form edges and bottoms fit tightly, or caulk the joints, or line the forms with plastic; a leak can leave pits and potholes on the formed concrete sides.

One bag of concrete mix fills two forms this size. Mix the concrete according to the directions on the bag and work it into the forms. Prod it thoroughly into all the corners, and tap the perimeter of the form with a hammer to work out all the air pockets. Scrape the excess concrete off the top of the form and leave it set for an hour or two before you trowel. If you trowel too soon, you'll bring too much water to the surface, leaving the concrete weak and flakey. Let it set until you can make

SIDE VIEW

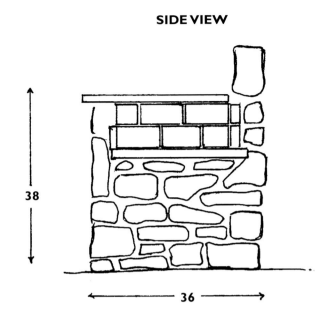

a thumbprint in the surface but can't push your thumb right in. Then smooth the surface with a trowel.

The concrete has to stay in the forms for two or three days to cure hard enough to move. Keep it damp and shady with a piece of plastic over the top to hold the moisture in. Concrete needs water to continue the chemical reaction which makes it hard.

While the countertops are curing, consider the foundation. The best and the easiest foundation is bedrock, or at least a big slab of Pre-Cambrian Shield that isn't going to flex and shift with the frost. Fortunately, there's a lot of that in cottage country. However, if the most convenient place to put the barbecue is on soft earth, you can make a slab of faux rock with concrete.

First, excavate the top 12" of soil, removing the roots and leaving the rocks. Then

STONE

Gather twice as much as you think you'll need. Not that there is anything wrong with your estimating skills. But you will appreciate having lots of rocks to choose from when it comes time to fit them into the puzzle. Any size will do, but big square chunks will be more useful than the abstract cannonballs. Set the best aside for corners. And save the very best, biggest, flattest slab for the upright heat reflector at the back. It's the most visible chunk of the barbecue—the part you pat and lean on while you tell your friends how you built this thing.

refill half the depth of the hole with 6" of rock or crushed stone. This is mostly for drainage, thus removing the water that would otherwise expand with frost and heave the barbecue around. Level the surface of crushed stone and tamp it.

Now build a form of 2 x 6s, slightly larger than the perimeter of the barbecue. Set the form on the crushed stone fill, square it, level it, brace it, and fill it with concrete, just as you did for the countertops. Don't bother to trowel, but do keep it shaded and damp.

Whether you built a slab foundation or

Build the firebox from heat-resistant bricks, and then fill in around it with stone.

started with bedrock, draw the perimeter dimensions on the surface with chalk. That's the outline on which to start the stonework.

Brush any debris off the base then slap a load of mortar along one edge. Keep it back a couple of inches from the chalk line, which represents the face or perimeter. And use a chopping motion to spread the mortar into a furrowed bed, 1-2" deep.

Set the first rock at a corner. Line up its two outer faces with the perimeter mark, and

tap the rock into position. Tap just enough to settle it into the mortar. You should see the mortar bulge a bit toward the face.

Set the second corner rock, then fill in the face between the two corners, bedding each rock into the mortar with a tap or two, keeping the faces plumb and aligned with the chalk perimeter. A straightedge or string, set corner to corner, will help. If the rock won't sit upright with its outer face plumb, shove a small rock shim underneath.

Try to match the tops of the rocks in each course. If they're all the same height—with no big steps from rock to rock—the next higher course will be a breeze to fit.

Lay out all four faces of the first course and then fill in behind them. For this particular barbecue, we left the center open to create a little storage cubby. A simpler variation would be four solid faces with a rubble core— unmortared—to let any water drain away. Drainage also requires that at least one of the vertical gaps in the bottom course be left open. Always assume that some water will get inside, and remember to leave an exit.

Fill the vertical joints in the bottom course by slicing mortar into the gaps from above. Let this bulge out toward the face, but don't try to clean it up. Then slap a layer of mortar on top of the first course to make a bed for the second course.

In the second and subsequent courses, bridge each joint in the course below. If each rock rests on two below, you'll span the gaps and stagger the vertical joints, making a

TOP VIEW

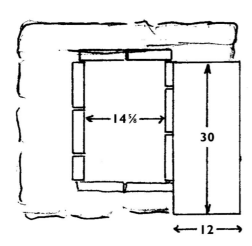

much stronger wall. This is considerably easier if the course below presents a flat top on which to build.

Each course proceeds in the same order:
1. Set the corners.
2. Fill in the faces between them.
3. Bridge the joints below.
4. Keep the tops as even as possible.
5. Fill in behind.
6. Stuff the vertical joints with mortar.
7. Lay a mortar bed for the next course.

As each course rises, check the corners to keep them plumb, and measure the height. Ultimately, we want to end up with the grill at 36" and a countertop at 38". Allowing 2" for the countertop plus mortar, plus 9" for two courses of firebrick, means we have to arrive at a flat base for the firebox at a 27"

height (27" + 9" + 2" = 38"). In this particular case, we also had to cap the little storage cubby with a precast concrete slab, so we stopped the stone base at 25" and laid the slab on top of that.

Don't be tempted to take a shortcut with the brick and form the firebox from stone. At best, the heat will crack the masonry. At worst, an exploding stone can injure the cook.

Wet the firebricks before you begin, and draw a precise outline of the firebox shape on the base. Use a wide "brick set" chisel to cut the bricks, or cut them to size with a masonry blade in the circular saw. Stand the bottom course on edge around the perimeter, just to get the fit right. Then cement them end to end with a slather of refractory cement. It's fast

HANGAR DETAIL

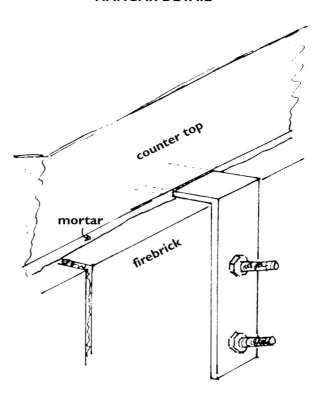

drying, so trowel off any excess cement as you go, and work quickly.

Butter the top of the first course with refractory cement, and set the second course, making sure to overlap the vertical joints, just as you did with the stone. And check the final dimensions at the top. The grill will have to

The firebox is designed to fit the grills.

fit down into the firebox, and we haven't left much room to spare.

While the firebox is setting, build around it with more stone. Maintain the same vertical faces we began from the bottom, and bring the top of the stonework up to the top of the firebox.

Use ordinary 4" steel corner braces for hangers. A couple of flathead bolts, with nuts on the front, provide rests for the grills. Set the hangers over the top edge of the firebox. Then mortar the countertops on top of that. Tap the countertops into position and level, then recheck the hangers, pushing them back into the mortar until they're tight against the side of the firebox.

The big stone at the back reflects a little heat onto the grill, but it's really there to deflect the wind. Some barbecues sport a little chimney at the back, but smoke still rises through the open grill and into the eyes of the cook. Forget the chimney.

Tidy builders will worry about the ragged bulge of mortar squeezing out between the stones. Don't try to clean it up until it has had a couple of hours to firm. Then use the point of the trowel to push the mortar back into the joint. You can trowel it flush with the face, or rake out the joint to a uniform, recessed depth. Use a narrow "pointing" trowel (or a wet, gloved finger) to smooth the recessed joints.

Cover the whole shebang with a sheet of plastic to keep the moisture in for three days. And then leave it for three weeks before getting the charcoal and burgers out. A layer of sand in the bottom of the firebox will protect the masonry bottom and will raise the coals closer to the grill.

Bon appétit.

Use ordinary steel corner braces for hangers. Flat-head bolts provide rests for the grills

HORSESHOE
PITS

Horseshoe pitching is one of those simple cottage games that always attracts a crowd and at least four different versions of the rules. The first debate is over the pitch itself—perhaps because it's such a casual game that the stakes are squeezed into whatever patch of grass remains open after parking, gardens, and clotheslines have staked their claims.

Officially, the two horseshoe stakes should be 40' apart. And each stake stands in the center of a pit of loose dirt or sand. The sand takes some of the bounce out of a flying 2 ½ pound shoe, ensuring that it stays more or less where it lands. The lack of certainty in that last sentence suggests that the entire pitch be located a safe distance from windows, cars, and unattended kids. And, if you have a choice, lay out the pitch on a north-south line, so nobody can use the old sun-in-the-eyes excuse. Locating on level terrain eliminates yet another excuse.

Each pit is 3' across and 4' wide. A simple rectangle of 2 x 6 or 2 x 4 lumber will

Dig out the turf to make a shallow pit of loose dirt or sand.

form the box. Pressure-treated lumber lasts longer than untreated, but it costs a little more. And remember that whatever you buy is going to spend the summer half-buried and regularly battered by flying steel. Under the circumstances, cheap is okay.

Overlap the ends of the lumber, as shown in the diagram, and secure each corner with two screws. The screws, of course, have less grip in the end grain than they would in the cross grain, so use longer 3" screws in these joints. Predrill the screw holes to prevent splitting.

Even with big screws, these open rectangles are going to flop and wobble until we get them in the ground. They don't need strength, but it will be handy to keep the corners square while we're moving them around. A couple of diagonal braces, nailed across the corners, will keep things in shape temporarily. When the pit is ready, we can turn the box over with the brace on the bottom and just leave it there, buried.

Dig the two shallow pits, just deep enough

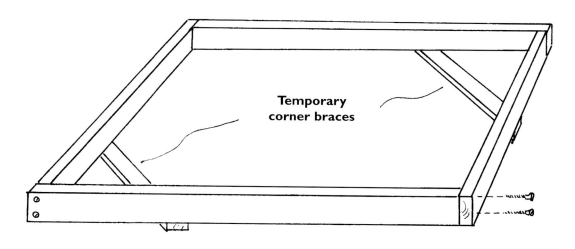

Temporary corner braces

The stake extends 14" above the sand, and leans towards the opponent's stake, 3" off vertical at the top.

to set the tops of the boxes flush with the surface. Set the boxes in place and line them up with one another. The stake, remember, will go in the middle, so the center of one box has to be 40' from the center of the other box. That leaves the front of one box 36' from the front of the other. When the boxes are in position, backfill around the outside edges to hold them in place.

You should now, in theory, be able to dump sand in the box, drive in the stake, and start to play. In theory. In real life, every off-the-shelf horseshoe set I've ever seen comes with a dinky, little 24" stake. The stake is supposed to have 14" sticking up out of the sand. Add 4" for the sand and there's only 6" of stake left to drive in the hard ground underneath. That's not enough to stand up

against the impact of hummingbird shoes. Full-bore, body-contact, let-er-rip horseshoes will knock that stake over like a lone blade of grass on the freeway. If you can't find a longer stake, dig a 6" hole in the bottom of the pit and set that store-bought stake in a shovelful of fresh concrete. Then dump the sand in the box and rake it level.

The stake, as I've said, protrudes 14" above the sand. But it doesn't stand up straight. It leans slightly toward the opponent's stake—3" off vertical at the top if anybody is being fussy (and you can bet your sweet bippy that somebody will be).

Leaners only count as one point, all the arguments notwithstanding.

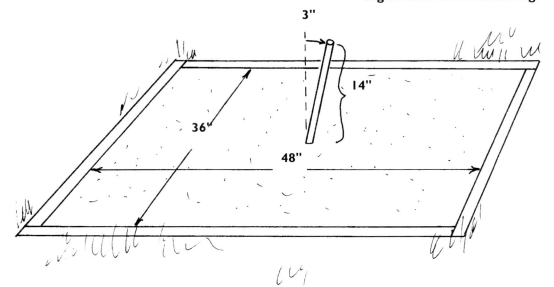

THE RULES

The first player stands beside one stake and throws two shoes to the far stake. Normally, a right-handed thrower will stand to the left of the box and take one long left-footed stride as part of the throwing motion. The step should not go beyond the real or imaginary foul line, 3' in front of the stake.

Then the second player throws two shoes from the same end. If there are only two players, they now walk to the far stake together, count the points, and throw the shoes back the way they came. With four players, the walk is eliminated. The two players standing at the far end count the points and throw the shoes back. Note that partners in team play stand at opposite ends. Opposing players share an end. This may be construed as being friendly with the competition or as keeping the other guy honest.

The object is to land the shoe around the stake. "Around" means that both tips of the shoe project beyond the stake. If you can touch both tips with a straightedge—without contacting the stake—that's a ringer. A ringer is worth three points.

Close also counts. A shoe that lands within 6" of the stake scores one point. And, since the standard horseshoe is 6" wide, measured from tip to tip, the test for a single point is to measure it with another horseshoe. If you can touch the stake with one tip and the disputed shoe with the other tip, then it's close enough for the single point.

That's it: one point or three. There is no two-point "leaner" in the official rules, despite what your opponents may say. A shoe in contact with the stake is either a ringer or a single point. Period.

A shoe that lands outside the box and then bounces or rolls into the box, doesn't count. No matter how close it is when it rolls to a stop. It can hula-hoop the stake three times and dance a jig on the top. Doesn't matter. It's dead.

Only one player can score in an end, and the points go to the player whose shoe is nearest to the stake. If each player throws a ringer, the ringer closer to the stake takes three. If there's a tie, the tied shoes cancel one another out, and the next closest shoe counts instead.

Normally, the team that scores in any one end is handicapped by throwing first in the next end. Throwing first is a disadvantage because your opponent can knock away your shoe with his. The maximum number of points in an end is six (if one player throws two ringers), and the game is played to 21, 40, or 50.

Yes, there are variations in the rules. That's where the disputes begin. Lightweight players may, by mutual consent, shorten the pitch from 40' to 30'. You may agree to count all points and limit the game to 20 ends. Some players drop the rule of "last scorer throws first" and alternate the lead instead. Feel free to invent your own cottage rules to suit the terrain and the players. But beware that when steel rings on stake—calling all within earshot to compete—part of the contest will be over the rules.

TIRE
SWING

A worn out tire has always been unwelcome on the road. There was a time, however, when the driver's bad news meant good news for the kids. The old-fashioned, recycled tire swing was simplicity itself. And yet, like many good ideas that have been around for a while, the tire swing has attracted a few improvements over the years.

The heritage approach was to tie one end of a rope around the tire and the other end over a sturdy branch. It worked, but you had to be small enough to fit inside the tire or big enough to pull yourself up onto the knot and swing with the tire underneath your thighs. Of course, there was always one daredevil who would swing standing up but usually without parental consent.

In, over, or standing up, there was no safe and comfy way to settle back and relax in the old-fashioned tire swing. There was no easy way to sit so long as the tire was suspended from a single knot. It was hanging up and down instead of on the flat.

Hanging a flat tire will require at least three points of suspension. Three mere loops of rope won't do because the tire changes shape every time a swinger mounts. When the rubber distorts, a rope loop can slip around the tire and leave it hanging from a single point again—up and down instead of flat.

Three eye bolts, spaced evenly around the perimeter, will solve the slippage problem and simplify future adjustments. A shank length of 2" will put the bolt through most tires. Do, however, use the biggest washer you can find.

ROPE

Rope comes in almost as many varieties as tires. Read the label before you buy. The label should rate the rope for holding strength, but you'll need something at least ½" thick. Natural hemp rope is rough on the hands. Some synthetics don't last long in sunlight. Some stretch. Nylon is strong and weather resistant but expensive.

Chains are more durable than rope but have a few problems of their own. They're harder to adjust than rope, and they present an added risk of pinched fingers.

If you choose a synthetic rope, you'll have to fuse any cut ends. If possible, have it cut to length at the store, where they likely have a heated wire just for this purpose. If you cut it at home, you can fuse the frayed ends with a small flame, but watch your hands. A drop of melted plastic on the skin can cause a nasty burn.

First, mark three spots around the circumference of the tire. The sidewall is the weakest part of the tire. We want the eye bolt in the thicker tread area. Not in the middle of the tread, however, but on the upper edge— the shoulder—where the rope will pull almost straight up from the eye bolt and not twist it sharply sideways.

Spacing can be done by eye. But if you want to challenge (or annoy) the kids with a little geometry, the circumference of a circle is always the diameter times pi (3.14). Pick a starting point on the shoulder of the tire and measure straight across the center to the opposite shoulder. That's the diameter. It would take 3.14 diameters to go all the way around the circle. So, measure off the same distance, except this time follow the perimeter instead of crossing the center of the circle. One diameter's distance from the starting point is almost a third of the way around the circle. Fudge it out by the width of your thumb (to make up for the 0.14), and it will be pretty darned close. With any luck, the kids will have forgotten your amazing shortcut by the time they get to high school and serious geometry.

Drill the holes with an ordinary high-speed bit. Don't wreck a good spade bit here. We want a bit that comes to a simple, conical point, not the one with sharp, pointed shoulders. Those are for boring tidy holes in wood. Here, just under the rubbery surface, we're going to hit a patch of fine steel wires (which is why they call tires "steel-belted"). The steel belt would rip the pointed shoulders off a woodworking bit. Use a cheap bit. You'll hear it when you hit the steel, but just press on through.

Now, if this were anything else but a tire, we could just slip the eye bolt through the hole. The tire, however, has a stubborn talent for closing a hole the moment you pull out the bit. Which is why the tire can run over a nail in the city and not go flat until you're at the cottage, 100 miles from the nearest garage.

Ream out the hole by running the bit through several times. Then screw the bolt into the hole. It will get tight. You might have to put

Fasten the rope to the eye bolt with an easily adjusted bowline knot.

a screwdriver through the eye and use the extra leverage to turn the bolt. Drive it right up to the eye, then put a large washer and a nut on the other end, inside the tire. A dab of varnish, or fingernail polish, will help keep the nut from working loose. With or without the varnish, check the nuts regularly to be sure that none are coming loose.

Traditionally, tire swings were tied to a stout branch belonging to the biggest tree in the yard. There's more to it than that. First, assume that at least one kid is going to fall off any swing. Check the landing area for rocks, uneven ground, and other hazards. Then consider the tree itself as a hazard, and determine whether the swing can be suspended far enough out on the limb that an exuberant swing can't smack somebody's noggin against the trunk.

Second, check the health of the tree. Has it got all its leaves? Any dead limbs farther out on the branch? Will it take the strain?

Drill holes for the eye bolts in the top shoulder of tread. The tire is thicker there than in the sidewall.

Finally, keep in mind that even a healthy branch can be mortally injured by the long-term wear and tear of a poorly attached swing. A rubbing rope can wear away bark and damage the vital sapwood. You can help by distributing the stress of the rope across a wider area with a pad or by passing several loose loops around the branch and through a ring. Most of the abrasive swinging action will wear on the ring instead of the branch. You can buy inexpensive steel rings wherever chain is sold. Even with a ring and a pad, move the point of support regularly and take the swing down in the fall.

Tie three ropes to the ring and then to the eye bolts on the tire, using nonslip bowline knots (see diagram). Three ropes offer some variety. You can tie them off at the same length for a flat, doughnut seat. Or shorten one rope to raise the tire at an angle. The high side provides a back for tired recliners—Lazy Boy meets the Michelin Man!

Choose a stout limb and suspend the swing from a ring, to reduce wear and tear on the bark.

With 3-ring suspension you can raise one side to make a recliner

KNOTTY PICTURE

The bowline makes a nonslip knot that's easy enough for the kids to tie...if you tell them about the frightened rabbit: He came out of his hole and had almost circled the tree, when he spotted a fox and dove headfirst back to safety.

Bowline knot

CLOSING TIPS

There's a reason for having our Labor Day in the fall. It's called closing the cottage, the weekenders' annual rite of work, that Te Deum of chores designed to defend a summer place against the coming onslaught of winter. It isn't winter's chill we worry about. It's the damage ice can do to plumbing and docks, the invading vermin, vandals, and Visigoths.

No wonder cottagers suffer last-mile whiplash in the spring, straining to see around the final bend after a too-long winter away. Has it burned to the ground? Collapsed under the snow? Is there a litter of skunks under the floor? Have the Visigoths smashed in the door? Is there anything in the city that is quite so tense as that final mile to the lake?

Winter's peace of mind depends on seeing to all the details in the fall. A checklist helps. Every cottage is different, and so every closing list will differ in the details, but the basics are the same:

1. Remove any valuables that might attract vandals.

2. Remove any food that might attract vermin.

3. Remove docks and boats from the water.

4. Remove the water from everything else.

PLUMBING

Before you drain any pipes, turn off the water heater at the panel (or at the valve if it's gas fired). Switch off the pump. Then open all the faucets, inside and out. Don't forget the shower and the laundry tubs. This lets air into the top of the system so the water can run out the bottom

Drain the hot-water tank through the outlet near the bottom. You might have to attach a hose to the outlet in order to drain the tank without flooding the cottage (keep the hose lower than the tank at all points). An older tank can become plugged with rust, minerals, or lake gunk. If the sediment clogs the outlet before the tank is completely empty, the water left behind might later freeze and split the tank. You can check by running the drain hose into buckets and monitoring the outflow. If your 30-gallon tank doesn't yield 30 gallons of water, you might want to clean the sediment out.

Drain the water softener, or any other tanks, just as you did the hot-water tank.

To drain the pipes, open all the in-line valves (turn them counterclockwise). And then remove the little pea-sized caps underneath the valves (they screw off counterclockwise), and put the caps someplace where you'll find them in the spring.

The in-line valves (also called "shutoff" valves, "stop" valves, or "straight

Remove the caps from beneath the in-line valves in order to drain the pipes.

stops") should be positioned at every low point in the system. If so, opening the faucets and removing the valve caps will empty the entire system on the cottage side of the pump. If not, you might have to blow out any undrained dips in the line with compressed air—or your lungs if it's only a short section of pipe.

To empty the other side of the system—between the pump and the water source—pull the intake pipe out of the water and open the footvalve. That's the odd-looking gizmo on the end that keeps the water in the pipe from running back into the lake. You can open the valve to drain the line or remove it completely. Clean out the summer collection of weeds and snails, and stow the footvalve away until spring. Finally, remove the intake pipe from the pump, clean the intake screen (if there is one), and grease any metal couplings (though most are plastic these days).

Now most of the trapped water is inside the pump itself, which, of course, would be the most expensive part to replace in spring. Remove all the plugs from the pump, including the primer plug, which may be part of the pressure gauge. Blow into the primer hole to force out any remaining water. Grease the plugs and store them for winter.

The pressure tank may need some special attention, depending on how it was mounted. If the connector

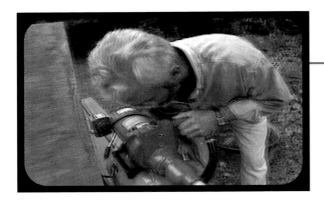

Remove all the plugs from the pump and blow into the primer hole to force out any remaining water.

(where the pipe goes in) is the lowest part of the tank and the tank is higher than the pump, the tank will automatically drain through the pump. If the tank is lower than the pump or mounted on its side, then you might have to detach the tank and tip it to drain.

Some of your appliances will have pumps, too. Those pumps, hidden inside the appliances, may be harder to drain than the main pump. If you have a washing machine or a dishwasher at the cottage, drain them if you can. If you can't, put a little RV antifreeze in the intake hose and flick on the machine just long enough to start the pump—sucking antifreeze into the pump and displacing the water that was there.

A good flush should empty the toilet tank. Hold down the handle to get all the water out, then look inside just to be sure. Flushing, of course, won't empty the bowl. Dip out the bowl as best you can, then replace the water in the trap with RV antifreeze.

The trap—that dip at the bottom of the bowl which refuses to empty—must always have liquid of some kind in it to keep the smelly gas in the septic tank from coming back up the pipe and into the bathroom. RV antifreeze is relatively benign. Don't use inappropriate, toxic substitutes which could disrupt the workings of the septic system with the first flush of spring.

There are similar traps under every drain in the cottage—sinks, tubs, showers, whatever. Unlike the toilet trap, these are readily accessible (under the sink, for example). Most have a removable cap at the bottom of the U. Unscrew the cap to drain the trap and, if necessary, to clean it. Then replace the cap, and refill the trap with a cup of RV antifreeze down the drain.

WILDLIFE

A critical part of the closing ritual takes aim at those critters who would love to move in when you move out. Bats, mice, and squirrels can wriggle in through the smallest, most unlikely holes. However, the ideal time to block all those little holes was last summer, when the critters were outside feeding. By now they could be inside sleeping, and a too-fastidious sealing will only ensure that when you come back in spring the beasts—plus babies and six months of droppings—will still be on the inside, along with an almighty smell!

By closing day, it is more important to

Empty the drain traps and re-fill them with RV anti-freeze.

remove any food that might attract new tenants or encourage the current ones to stay. Empty the cupboards and the fridge. Clear the crumbs from under the toaster and the soap from the shower. Take any pet food or leftover seeds.

One easily forgotten critter entrance is the chimney. Starlings and raccoons regard it as an open door. If you close the woodstove and the fireplace flue, you can keep the wannabe Santas out of the cottage itself, but you might still find a mess or a body in the flue by spring. The best chimney defense is up on the roof. Wire a sturdy mesh across the top of the flue to keep them out. Some commercial rain caps for chimneys come enclosed at the sides with a mesh "spark arrestor." It arrests break-and-enter birds and bandit coons as well as sparks.

The big "B & E" culprits are bears. They're primarily attracted to food but aren't averse to smashing a window or a door just to go in and check out the cupboards. Cottagers in bear country learn to cover doors and windows with grilles or solid shutters.

If there are porcupines in the neighborhood, the fall food cleanup includes the outdoors. Porkies will chew up anything with a salty taste, even radiator hoses and glue. They'll eat axe handles, plywood, and paddles if you don't put them away.

SECURITY

The two-legged pests aren't so easily deterred. Good deadbolt locks will help. So will shutters if you have them. Insurers against such things advise that intruders often

PLUMBING

√ Turn off the water heater.
√ Switch off the pump.
√ Open all the faucets.
√ Drain the hot-water tank.
√ Drain the water softener and other tanks.
√ Open all the in-line valves.
√ Remove the drain caps underneath the valves.
√ Blow out any undrained dips in the line.
√ Pull the intake pipe out of the water.
√ Open the footvalve.
√ Remove the intake pipe from the pump.
√ Clean the intake screen.
√ Grease any metal couplings.
√ Remove all the plugs from the pump.
√ Blow into the primer hole to force out any remaining water.
√ Grease the plugs and store them for winter.
√ Drain all the appliance pumps or fill them with RV antifreeze.
√ Flush the toilet to empty the tank.
√ Dip out the toilet bowl.
√ Replace the water in the bowl with RV antifreeze.
√ Drain the traps under the sinks and tubs.
√ Refill the traps with RV antifreeze.

don't go in if they can't see in. You can also insure against vandalism and theft, but coverage is costly on unattended property.

Perhaps the best way to quit worrying and to enjoy the winter is to take any valuables with you. That includes tools, outboard motors, appliances, and pricey portables. Also potables. Liquor would not only be a loss in itself. It might inspire additional mayhem.

The best form of security, and every cottager's most valuable asset, is friendly year-round neighbors who won't mind keeping an eye on things. Put them at the top of every cottage closing list.